D0426685

O and AN EMPTY ROOM

These two verse plays break new ground in their attempts
to find a language to communicate states of mind and
different intellectual concepts. O, which is written in a
series of 'speakies', has an overall effect that is bizarre
and disturbing, utilising as it does arresting new techniques
to evoke the quality of the communication between the in-
terior voices of different characters. On another level it
is also a biting satire on Swedish concepts of 'liberalism'
and 'welfare', and middle-class conformity. An Empty Room
communicates the weird corporate atmosphere of different
aspects of a place in twelve strongly etched 'pictures'.

Sandro Key-Aberg is a brilliant young Scandinavian poet and
dramatist whose experiments with language and dramatic
form as tools of a deeper, more meaningful communication
make him a genuine exponent of that much overworked
phrase 'avant-garde drama'. The plays have been imagin-
atively translated by Brian Rothwell and Ruth Link.

PLAYSCRIPT 28

'o' &
'an empty room'

sandro key-aberg

TRANSLATED BY BRIAN ROTHWELL
& RUTH LINK

CALDER AND BOYARS · LONDON

First published in Sweden 1965
by Bonniers Publishing House, Stockholm

(c) Bonniers Publishing House 1965

First published in Great Britain 1970
by Calder and Boyars Ltd
18 Brewer Street, London W1R 4AS

(c) Sandro Key-Aberg 1970

These translations

(c) Calder and Boyars Limited 1970

ISBN 0 7145 0735 0 Cloth Edition
ISBN 0 7145 0736 9 Paper Edition

Printed by photo-lithography
and made in Great Britain at
The Pitman Press, Bath.

CONTENTS

O was first performed at the Stadstheater, Stockholm, 1965, with the following cast:

A.   Olof Thunberg
B.   Gerd Hagman
C.   Hakan Serner
D.   Lena Granhagen
       Nils Eklund
       Lean Soderblom

The roles of A, B, C and D were alternated by the actors in each speaky.

The play was directed by Claes Rettig

This translation of O, adapted by H. B. Fortuin, was broadcast on the BBC Third Programme on January 12th 1968, with the following cast:

A.   Anthony Jackson
B.   Catherine Dolan
C.   Timothy Bateson
D.   Max Adrian

The roles of A, B, C and D were alternated by the actors in each speaky.

The play was directed by H. B. Fortuin

(TEXT A is shown on a screen in front of the stage.
The text runs across it like in a news-flash. Simul-
taneous COMMENTARY to the text comes from a
microphone at the back of the theatre; unclear, irri-
tating and irritated.

TEXT B is spoken while there are pictures on the
screen; city-scenes and advertisements (enlarged).
Noise of traffic)

TEXT A.   I'm so bored at home
                    Am I too young to go with a boy?
                    Is this love?
                    Is it WRONG to be so old?
                    Am I too young?
                    I want to be a lady cop
                    What's the right present?
                    Should I talk to my daughter?
                    Dad won't say yes.
                    I want to be a pal
                    Why are men such swine?
                    How should one behave?
                    Who speaks to whom?
                    I don't dare to show myself
                    Is it really fair?
                    Drink milk with your dinner
                    I'm fed up with nagging about marriage
                    Earplugs help
                    Tell them how long you're staying
                    Don't wear your heart on your sleeve
                    Bribing the kids a defeat for Mum
                    Look after your pets
                    Do you only speak English?
                    How different it can be

I can't stand my neighbour
Going bald at 17
Is money everything?
Tell them, Mum
Cyclists
Where is it?
Where has politeness gone?
Get out into the country
Does Mum want to be alone?
Think of something else
Our boy is different
It's so horrible being alone.
I can't find my best friend
Shall I break off?

(Commentary for TEXT A)

Oh, oh what's all this about then?
Oh yeah suppose that'd be a bit more fun,
   wouldn't it
Well Christ, in the name of sanity, what
   questions! I've
not seen any love lying around here anyway that
I haven't! pschaw asking questions like
   that!
crass stupidity
Jeese just these mad questions all the time
I suppose it's meant to be one of these
   new sorts of poetry
or something.
And what use poetry might be
I've never understood
you bloody well ought to be able to say
   straight out what it's all about
instead of going on with all these snide
   allusions
Pure unadulterated lunacy that's what it is
It's these bloody egg-heads
Now who's thought this one up
Should tell us how long they intend keep-
   ing it up instead
Not one single bloody joke at all

Try asking them what they mean by all
  this
and of course the only answer you get is:
mean mean, we don't mean anything; it's
  art, art
As soon as there's something any ordinary
  human-being
can't understand, that's art.
Do they really think you can answer all
  this,
dammit there isn't one sensible question
  in the whole thing.
Or of course it's some bloody sort of irony
if you can't understand a load of shit.
You won't be able to talk like an ordinary
  human-being soon
Without someone coming along and being
  funny at your expense.
Yes indeed they could all do with a wet-
  nurse to look after them.
Oh no! what the hell's this coming now?
Ach kiss me behind and come back beating
  your drum and blowing
your trumpet.
Now what is this all about really, what
  bloody mum?
Think about something else. I'll think
  about what the hell I want
Oh Christ yes, very profound I'm sure all
  this, of course.
Who the hell's our boy. I haven't got a boy.
Oh yes, now they're going to start being
  sensitive as well.
Now they'll start talking about death any
  minute too.
That's really popular after all that is.
Well look at the bugger, didn't I tell you.

TEXT B.   Noises in the ears
                 Running eyes
                 Sores in the rectum
                 Bent nails
                 Eczema from gold

Dyed hair
Unpleasant smell
Fat legs
Brown spot
Big nose
Swollen veins
Drooping Hair-tufts
Sticky hair
Fat cheeks
Perpetual cold
Too fat
Headache
Period pains
Heavy perspiration
Colour-blind
Varicose veins
Inner tubes
Heart murmur
Near-sighted
Knobby elbows
Undeveloped breast
Ingrown toe-nails
Blushing
One leg shorter
Disappointed in Beauty Institutes
Foot-cramp
Ears that stick out
Menstrual injections
Incipient moustache
Fallen arches
Belching
Stomach ache
Embarrassing hair
Crazy as a flat earther
A British Life.

(When the curtain rises for the first speaky
Pillar - A - a weak yellow light
Screen - B - an intense dark-blue
The set otherwise is satin drapes, black.

The actors enter carrying iron garden seats painted
with luminous paint so that they show in the dark;

they put the chairs in a row and sit bestraddling them.
The stage gets slowly brighter. The chairs are put
away in different parts of the stage.

Alternatively the first speaky can be performed in the
audience, the actors coming up through the audience
from different parts of the theatre)

FIRST SPEAKY

A.   Well, what are you doing here?

B.   Imagine bumping into you!

C.   How very nice to see you

B.   How very nice to see you

A.   How very nice to see you

D.   How very nice to see you
    What a pleasant surprise to see you here

A.   Well then and how are you?

B.   Oh not too bad you know, jogging along

C.   and how are you getting on?

D.   dragging along by my teeth and my nails
    an inch at a time

C.   and you're getting on?

D.   Oh yes bit of bleeding in the gums other-
      wise everything's fine

C.   Nice to hear that, really nice

D.   Nice to hear that, really nice

A.   Nice to hear that, really nice

B.   Nice to hear that, really nice
      How are you; how are you getting on?

D.   Oh happy as a sandboy, happy as a sandboy

B.   Well that's the way the cookie crumbles

A.   Getting along like a house on fire

C.   The timbers creak
      and thunder and roar

A.   Oh really I didn't know that

B.   And everything's quite alright?

D.   Oh really I can't complain
      Operation last month no good at all
      Otherwise everything's fine

B.   Really nice to hear that

A.   That's nice, nice to hear that

C.   That's nice, nice to hear that

A.   And you're feeling hale and hearty?

C.   Indeed I am cancer in the stomach
      My heart in my mouth
      But can't really complain

A.   Well, it's nice to hear that, really nice

C.   Well, it's nice to hear that, really nice

D.   Well, it's nice to hear that, really nice

B.   Well, it's nice to hear that, really nice

D.   I'm very glad you turned up

14

A.	Same here, old chap, same here
C.	grand that you managed to come
B.	Glad you could get away
A.	How very nice to see you all
B.	just like old times
C.	<u>We</u> can always pass the time somehow
B.	Sure enough we can kill time together
A.	Kill weary time that we never get enough of
B.	forget death while we wait for life
C.	forget life waiting for death
D.	I'm sure we've always got something to talk about
A.	should think <u>so</u>
B.	I'd think so too
C.	I'd think so too
D.	I'd think so too
B.	a few sweet nothings, eh?
C.	You've always got something saved for a rainy day
D.	yes, you've always something you want to say
C.	Nice, really nice to hear that
B.	Nice, really nice to hear that

A.   Nice, really nice to hear that

D.   Nice, really nice to hear that

B.   Good Lord, just like it was

A.   Well then are we ready to start?

B.   Sure just blow the horn and we're off

A.   foot down and begin then?

B. C. D.   O.K.

(The change to the second scene is shown by the
actors going round the pillar A; props can be kept
behind this; and they change from caps to hats.
Pillar - A in this scene strong, yellowish
Screen - B strong, intense green colour (emerald)
Just before the actors begin they freeze while a notice
is lowered over the stage on which is written:

ACT I   THE BRIGHT MOMENTS OF LIFE

SECOND SPEAKY

A.   Life is sweet

B.   life is glorious

C.   it's really glorious and sweet

D.   it's delightful

A. B. C. D.   life is glorious and good

B.   we're positive people

A. C. D.   we're bloody positive

A.	Compared with us M.R.A.'s just piddling about
C.	A real Englishman is positive really
D.	But look we're well positive
C.	Well what are you talking about?
D.	I mean positive well ...
C.	Christ you do go on
D.	I mean well what are you like when you're positive?
C.	Well that's got nothing to do with it, has it? The question is if you should be positive or not You don't mean you question that one should be
D.	Oh not at all I'm as positive as hell, I am
C.	Well, very well then
A. B.	We are open to life in a simple way
C. D.	life's bloody marvellous
D.	we praise life
C.	we praise the mother country and the royal family
B.	parliament Wilson and all the party leaders
A.	Peace and co-operation between the nations
B. C. D.	A-ah! Yes!
A.	We praise love

B.	Which conquers all
C.	What?
B.	All
C.	Yeah but bloody hell you don't know that
B.	Oh now don't start arguing For Pete's sake we've agreed on this
D.	you must be loyal, dammit
C.	O.K. then let's say all
A.	So we praise love that conquers all
B.	that conquers all, that is
C.	we praise truth
D.	good lord yes
A.	definitely
B.	there's no doubt at all about truth
A. B. C. D.	we really are for truth
A.	used in the right way
B.	of course, and at the right time
C.	musn't be overdone
D.	for then truth becomes false
A. B. C. D.	absolutely
D.	And freedom for heaven's sake we praise freedom
C.	well obviously that goes without saying

18

B.   freedom as an absolute principle

A.   Certainly who says it should
                     apply in the individual case

B.   for someone who's positive
                     life always means freedom

A.   absolutely

D.   nice to hear you say that

A.   straight speaking when it's called for

D.   positive people are great

C.   It's only a bad man's negative

B.   No need to be so negative about everything

A.   After all if society hadn't all the faults it
                     has
                     it couldn't get any better

B.   and a better society is what we all want

C.   these gloomy views about everything

D.   Like the lack of doctors and the crowded
                     hospitals
                     we know most sick people aren't sick at all

A.   now the sick can be
                     as healthy as they like with impunity

C.   I think we should consider it a human right
                     to be on a waiting list (pause)

B.   I think every human being should have a
                     right
                     to be on every waiting list

D.   the wonderful thing about a lot of people

19

being worse off
is that such a lot of people will be better off

A.   and it's better thac we want things to be, isn't
it?

B.   just think how many people are better off
because others are worse off

C.   you know, I like the atom bomb
good lord life's more exciting with it
I think there must be a bit of danger in life
if you're really going to enjoy it, don't you?

D.   life should really go with a swing

A.   we praise man

B.   we'd almost forgotten that completely

C.   we praise the British man

D.   Yes, exactly

A.   the British in man

B.   We praise Brown Gillian Brown Patrick
Brown J. Brown
Billy Brown Jean Brown Walter Brown
Agnes
Brown Jeremiah Brown George

A. C.   We praise Clarke Mary Clarke Clarissa
Clarke Leonard
Clarke Veronica Clarke Jim Clarke Ronald
Clarke Sarah
Clarke Margaret Clarke William Clarke
Dave

D. B.   We praise Johnson James Johnston Thomas
Johnston Mildred
Rosemary Johnston Linden Johnston Jeremy
Johnston Brian
Johnston Max Johnston Hank

20

B. C.	We praise Williams Derek Williams
	   Fenella Williams Roland
	Williams William Williams Bert Williams
	   Harry Williams
	Myrtle Williams Theodore Williams
	   Audrey

A. B. C.	We praise Mac Millan Roger Mac Millan
	   Fred Mac Millan Dorothy
	Mac Millan Mac Mac Millan Sandra Mac
	   Millan Ian Mac Millan
	Violet Mac Millan Louise Mac Millan
	   Martin

C. B. D.	We praise Jones Robert Jones Norma Jones
	   Georgina
	Jones Desmond Jones Penelope Jones-
	   Jones
	Bob Jones Taffy Jones Tony

A. B. C. D.	We praise Smith Samuel Smith Kenneth
	   Smith Adam
	Smith Pat Smith Gwendoline Smith Mary-
	   Anne
	Smith John Smith Jonathan Leslie Smith
	Geraldine Smith-Smith
	Benedict

A. B. C. D.	we praise the buggers one and all
A.	we don't even forget the meanest author
B.	they're men of honour every one of them, they're all good people
C.	we think evil of no-one we have good faith in the good for we are what people should be like
D.	we believe in the future
A.	we believe in life for the living and the dying

B.	we believe in man
A. B. C. D.	it's not nice to think evil of man
C.	there's some good even in the worst
D.	there's no evil even in a bad man
A.	evil is nothing more than an illusion
B.	we won't say an evil word about anyone
C.	it's possible that some particular individual can have some particular little shortcoming but in that case it's only a mistake
D.	due to your not seeing properly
A.	No there are no real lunatics
B.	one or two eccentrics, perhaps
C.	yes or characters rather
D.	I'd prefer to talk about unusually constituted personalities
C.	or people with peculiar tendencies perhaps
B.	damn fools in fact
A.	but of course the expression damn fools taken completely without any evaluative connotation
B.	bloody fuckers
A.	but in that case understood only as a descriptive phrase
B.	(whispers)
C.	what!!

22

someone hit you over the head with a peg?

B.   (whispers)

C.   oh a truncheon
well you could have said that at first

B.   (whispers)

C.   I just don't believe it
people just don't do that

D.   what did he say?

C.   (whispers)

D.   Impossible an action like that
is something a man just wouldn't be guilty
    of

A.   what did he say?

D.   (whispers)

A.   quite out of the question that anyone would
    behave like that

C.   it's obvious that no-one
deliberately does harm to anyone else

A.   What a hatred for man to assert that
    someone
would want to cause pain to someone else

D.   what do you think it would look like if
    someone
deliberately hurt someone else
There's something cruel in assertion

A.   assertion is violation

D.   assertion is forcing people
to understand something

B.   Ah well when all's said and done
It was all my fault
After all there was no need for me to feel
    hurt
when they hit me

A.   exactly you don't need to suffer
just because someone's hurting you

C.   No need to care about little things like that

D.   Good lord you ought to think of it like a
    sort of traffic accident
on the narrow path of good-will

B.   yes you're right yes

A. B. C. D.   don't think we're against change

A. B.   we're really progressive people
as long as it's right

C.   the progress that is

D.   right?

A.   yes right

D.   what do you mean right?

A.   don't you know what right is?
God but you're hopeless!
What shall I say then
good changes, eh?

D.   good changes yes of course now I get it

A. B. C. D.   so we are for good changes

B.   everything good we are for

C.   we believe in the happiness of man

D.	we believe in the power of truth
A.	we believe in the strength of love
B.	we look forwards
C.	towards all the life that is waiting
A.	we look up
B.	we look down
D.	we look at everything upside-down
A. B. C.	No no we look up first and then we look down and everywhere it's life we see
D.	but wait a sec what did I say then?
A. B. C.	we look at mankind and love it
D.	no but wait a minute I'm lost
A. B. C.	we look at life and love it
D.	I don't understand where have you got to now?
A. B. C.	we look at everything with love
D.	No but listen where are you Wait a second please can't you go over that again? You, can't you listen I didn't follow that I tell you Dammit why can't you wait?

(After the second speaky, actors round the pillar A.
Scene in a wood in summer on screen B.
Bird-song, sound of breeze in loudspeakers.
Actors spray scent into the auditorium)

THIRD SPEAKY

A.   the sun, see the sun
        how it shines through the trees

B.   There's something beautiful about the
          moss under the trees, isn't there?

C.   and the wind the incomprehensible wind
        telling the old, old story in the treetops

D.   god yes gabbling away like mad

C.   and summer, wonderful summer
        with its nights
        white and fragile as old linen

B.   just think of an august afternoon in the
          cherry orchard

A.   do you remember how we gorged
        it was absolutely tremendous

B.   isn't there something beautiful
        about the light of a summer's day over
          the rolling hills of England?

D.   good as a pint

A.   just wandering at will

B.   being really close to nature

A.   you know it's nice, really nice

C.   you really feel the grass under foot

B.   and the flowers which bow before the wind

C.	now one should be really happy you know
A.	yes indeed that's all that's missing
B.	what does that matter it's times like this that make you feel you're really alive
C.	yes and life feels so real, don't you think?
D.	Well shall we be getting on then
B.	what's that what are you looking at?
A.	darling what's that you've got there?
B.	look she's got a bird
A.	oh look it's a little dead bird
D.	Oh yes yes she's got a little dead bird in her hand
B.	Oh no look it's completely dead
B.	poor, poor little bird so beautiful and so dead
A.	just think how cruel life can be at times
C.	feel how lovely and soft he is
B.	lovely little bird so lovely very lovely you can be though you're dead
D.	ah come on now and stop standing here moaning
A.	what do you mean standing moaning?
D.	there's nothing wonderful about a dead bird is there hundreds of birds die every day

C.	Ohh how cynical you are
B.	surely you still ought to show a bit of respect for death?
A.	you shouldn't say things like that surely you know that even a bird represents a part in life
C.	even this little bird lived a life of light and shade even this little bird has once loved
D.	well what's that got to do with it? love between birds what's that? human beings or horses copulating now that's quite something but birds, a bit of a fluttering, what's that?
A.	what the hell are you saying are you sneering at love?
C.	oh how cruel you are
B.	is a part of life so meaningless to you?
D.	Ah stop going on like that throw the bloody bird away to hell and come on
C.	don't touch me murderer
A.	surely you ought to show some respect for life
B.	you're trying to make fun of us perhaps
C.	I can't imagine how anyone can be so inhuman
A.	haven't you an ounce of feeling in your body?
C.	you haven't a heart that's for certain

A.   pity the bird isn't alive so you could
kill it isn't it!

B.   that's what you enjoy, eh
tormenting others?

A.   bloody fascist

C.   it makes me sick listening to you

A.   shut his trap for him

B.   a beating that's what you need

D.   ah stop arsing about

A.   we're not arsing about by god

B.   take that and shut up

A.   boot him one in the face dammit

C.   in the crotch too that hurts

B.   up and at him for king and country

A.   he's getting away the bugger

B.   let him blasted well go

A.   as long as we don't have to see him again

B.   don't stand there looking stupid
clear off out of our sight

A.   glad we got rid of him

B.   a nasty type when you think of it

A.   really disgusting I'd say

C.   how can a human-being be like that?

B.   it's like suddenly standing face
      to face with evil itself

A.   it was really good to
      show him his place

C.   it was the right thing to do

A.   yes by god it was the only right thing

B.   one simply shouldn't tolerate such people

C.   but how can human-beings be so heartless
      and unfeeling?

A.   one must fight evil wherever it appears

B.   whether it's a question of South Africa or
      the individual
      human-being one must show that one wants
      right

A.   if you're able to beat evil
      then you must attack evil

B.   take the opportunity when you have the
      upper hand
      when you're several against one

C.   yes, after all, otherwise you can't oppose
      evil

A.   indeed no, it's no use fighting then

B.   after all then you only get a beating

C.   yes after all there's no sense in that

A.   anyway he was a really nasty type

B.   horrible

(The sign is lowered again over the stage, it says:

30

ACT 2   ONE DAY IN LIFE

(The screen red, the pillar green
Between the speakies the set is changed in darkness
In the darkness very simple change of set especially
with the chairs; perhaps simple change of clothes
behind the pillar.

During the speakies pictures on the screen.

4th Speaky	breakfast things or furniture
5th Speaky	type-writers
6th Speaky	lunch-canteen in a factory
7th Speaky	street-scenes
8th Speaky	restaurant
9th Speaky	a lounge in a home
10th Speaky	bedroom in a home
11th Speaky	pictures of stars at night - with 2 proj-

ectors one can gradually bring out the picture of the
rails leading off into the distance to accompany the
speaky.

Appropriate sounds for each talkie are used to
"punctuate" them i.e. at the beginning and end of
each.)

FOURTH SPEAKY

A.   what did you say?

B.   do you want sugar I said

A.   if I want what was that?

B.   sugar I said

A.   if I want sugar?

B.	yes can't you hear me, you deaf or something?
A.	of course I can hear you
B.	well do you want sugar?
A.	don't shout your bloody head off
B.	well you can answer when I ask
A.	ask what then
B.	I said do you want sugar?
A.	bloody nag nag nag
B.	that's got nothing to do with it
A.	what's got nothing to do with what?
B.	the sugar with the nagging
A.	well for christ's sake I never said it had
B.	oh you're hopeless
A.	well did I say it or didn't I?
B.	oh Lord are you going to start again
A.	did I say it or didn't I?
B.	of course if I didn't say it then you didn't say it
A.	you see
B.	well what should I see now?
A.	that I was right
B.	have I said anything different then?

A.	no but you're sitting there looking smug
B.	my dear I take it all back
A.	well am I right?
B.	oh it's quite hopeless you twist everything I say inside out
A.	bloody nonsense is bloody nonsense even if you twist it to kingdom come
B.	well then let's say it was stupid
A.	let's say it was bloody nonsense I say
B.	oh very well then it's bloody nonsense
A.	must you look so miserable and sour about it?
B.	oh stop going on like this all the time
A.	just think if only you could control your- self and calm down
B.	I'm sorry but I get so sore when you go on at me like that
A.	be like a normal human-being then and speak English so you can be understood
B.	yes dear, now would you like sugar
A.	just a minute haven't I heard that some- where before?
B.	but I only want to be nice and thoughtful
A.	thoughtful! if I want sugar I'll take sugar can't you get that into your skull?

33

B.	I'm sorry
A.	there's bloody well nothing to be sorry about
B.	there now you've knocked the coffee over
A.	oh
B.	oh it's scalding hot oh oh
A.	you bloody well ought to watch out

FIFTH SPEAKY

A.	what a stuck-up shit that fellow Smith is isn't he?
B.	maybe
A.	you know there's something about that type ...
B.	well I haven't really thought about it
A.	there's something damnably oily and evasive you know a real Uriah Heep, that's what he is a real Uriah Heep
B.	oh I don't know
A.	no no but it's bloody well true all the same by the by has it ever struck you that his name's Ephraim, eh? wouldn't surprise me if he was a jew
B.	well that doesn't necessarily follow at all
A.	I said it wouldn't surprise me I said

34

I didn't say he was a jew

B.   jew jew doesn't matter at all if he is a jew

A.   have I said it does?
you think I'm an antisemitist, eh?

B.   I haven't said that at all

A.   said and said but you thought
thought there's one of those antisemitists
   sitting there, eh?

B.   but my dear fellow I didn't think that at all
I promise you

A.   O. K. we'll drop the subject but I can't help
being so damned annoyed when you're
   accused
of things like that
for god's sake it's hardly my fault he's a
   jew

B.   for heaven's sake I've never accused you

A.   now don't start again
you know it's only that soon you won't be
   able to speak
your mind in this country
soon you won't be allowed to say that a jew
   is a jew
even if he is a jew, dammit

B.   well it's hardly quite like that

A.   O. K. just you try pointing out the way
   things really are
and you'll see it doesn't matter a damn
   what it's about

B.   oh well surely you're exaggerating a bit

A.   you know as well as I do

that some people are untrustworthy some
   aren't
that some people are mean others aren't
that a few are talented others aren't
that some suit their job and some don't
that's just how things are
fucking hypocrisy to say anything else

B.   but what's that got to do with jews?

A.   damnation I haven't said
          it has to do with the jews

B.   then what are you talking about then?

A.   for christ's sake I haven't said a word
             about the jews

B.   maybe but even if someone's a bit
          unreliable he can still be a good person

A.   what do you really mean really?
          for christ's sake I haven't been sitting in
             judgement on people
          I've only said they were different
          surely you must at least agree
          that they're different some of them?

B.   of course everyone's not the same

A.   well then what are you quarreling about
          you know quite well I don't mean Smith's
          a bad person
          what I've said and still do is that he's
             different
          that's all

B.   I know I know

A.   can he help having too little experience
          two years less than me for example?
          of course he must compensate somehow
          for what he lacks in other ways

anyway surely that's obvious

B.   oh I think he does his job pretty well
                anyway

A.   now there you go again with your accusations
           for christ's sake I haven't said that he isn't
           good enough for his job
           have I I'm just asking you have I?

B.   but I didn't say that

A.   no no but it sounded as though you thought
                so

B.   I promise you I didn't at all

A.   no maybe not but you mustn't keep on
           jumping on me for all sorts of things
           I never said
           as for the jews
           I know as well as the next man
           that one or two of them
           had a hard time during the war in Germany

B.   had a hard time you can say that again

A.   but after all the thing's got to be looked at
                historically you know
           it was something that had to happen

B.   but for heavens sake that can't ...

A.   yeah, yeah I know what you're going to say
           but dammit I'm not trying to defend
           the way they were treated
           of course what happened was horrible
           specially for the jews themselves
           but you must learn to think about the thing
                historically
           dammit the germans themselves were
           victims of circumstances too

B.   but surely you can't

A.   ah stop sitting there looking so bloody
              morally at it
            you know as well as I do that the blame
              wasn't
            anyones in particular

B.   of course but I mean you can't get away
              from the fact
            that human-beings suffered

A.   of course not but listen
            you know if you look at the whole thing a
              bit more calmly
            isn't all the talk about that rather
              exaggerated, isn't it?
            isn't it always the way
            that the conquered are slandered?

B.   I just don't know what to say

A.   Besides you know,
            wasn't there a bit of life about the whole
              thing too
            Hitler was really quite a lad
            if you really think about it
            don't you think so?

            SIXTH SPEAKY

A.   the soup wasn't bad anyway was it?

B.   the soup was good, very good

A.   you were saying something about co-operation
              factory democracy or
            something

B.   yes I think its got the future on its side

A.   you think so

B.   well don't you think so?
38

A.   I don't believe in factory democracy for a
                minute

B.   don't you ?

A.   nope
                the bacon wasn't bad then, eh?

B.   oh the bacon's good, very good

A.   have another there's plenty

B.   oh I don't know

A.   go on, have another piece
                no use keeping it

B.   let me think about it

A.   don't you like bacon?

B.   oh yes of course I like bacon

A.   have some more then for god's sake

B.   O.K. throw me over another piece

A.   that's what I like to hear
                good food and fresh air never hurt anyone

B.   look here why don't you believe in factory
                democracy?

A.   I don't think it's the whole story

B.   well that's still no answer

A.   make people democratic first for christ's
                sake
                then maybe I'll start to believe in it

B.   but factory democracy is a way to make
        people democratic don't you see?

A.   sure sure it's some sort of infernal machine
                         that makes angels of them

B.   no of course I don't mean that

A.   look let me tell you what it's really like
                         no matter how co-operatively democratic
                            you made every
                         damn factory there'd always be someone
                         who got the power into his hands
                         all the power and nothing but the power

B.   oh I don't know really

A.   but I do
                         why don't you have some more bacon?
                         you've only had three pieces dammit

B.   that's plenty for me thanks

A.   if someone says he likes bacon
                         then he eats bacon

B.   yes but I'm full

A.   you only had one plate of soup
                         then you can bloody well manage a bit of
                            bacon

B.   you sound so damned mad

A.   hell I'm not damned or mad either
                         I just can't stand people who refuse
                         just because it's supposed to be refined
                            or something
                         People should take dammit
                         when it's offered

B.   yes but I'm full absolutely full
                         surely I can't help being full

A.   well maybe
                         besides democracy's against human nature

that's the long and the short of it

B.   human nature well I don't know

A.   look have you ever met one single human-
being
who'd refuse something so someone else
would do better?

B.   but that's just the reason why ...

A.   of course it's quite obvious that I'm not
against democracy
it's just that I'm for the elite
it's quite obvious that we're better some
of us
no, you know, the only way in which democracy can exist
is through some form of dictatorship
society must be led consistently and
absolutely firmly
by the elite so that democracy can be
assumed
democracy by force is the only thing which
lasts

B.   but then you can hardly talk of democracy

A.   what the hell do you think democracy is
then?
to bugger off and play hop-scotch when
you're needed for production?

B.   well hardly that exactly

A.   O.K. t hen
it's only people who're jealous
talk about equality
if you want the last piece of bacon take it

B.   no no thanks all the same

A.   O.K. then I'll have it

B.	yes just you take it
A.	O. K. don't have it then you'll be sorry later
B.	I'm full absolutely choc-a-bloc really
A.	no but of course you think I'm too fat of course it's bloody annoying you shouldn't be fat you shouldn't be intelligent soon there'll be a fucking law against being stupid as well what are you allowed to be in this bloody country
B.	you can really make mountains out of molehills can't you

A.	shall we call the wee waitress over, eh?
	look anyway you must have
	learnt to stuff a bit more bacon into you
	    next time
	you look like the seven hungry years for
	    god's sake.

SEVENTH SPEAKY

A.	it's torn
B.	torn?
B.	yes the ticket's torn
B.	I don't understand
A.	don't you see? a bit of the ticket's missing isn't there anymore, it's gone disappeared
B.	well what difference does that make?

42

A.   I can only accept complete tickets

B.   yes but it hasn't been used

A.   oh do you think you'd be able to travel on it
        if it were used?

B.   well you know of course I don't mean that

A.   it sounded like you did

B.   I just mean that the bit that's missing
           went with the other half

A.   you should have seen that it didn't

B.   but it was just a mistake

A.   that's your look-out not mine

B.   yes but I said to the conductor
        look there's a bit torn off
        doesn't matter he said

A.   what he says is his business

B.   don't the same rules apply on all buses then?

A.   I'm only allowed to accept complete tickets

B.   how can other conductors accept them then?

A.   that's a matter between you and the company

B.   god what a ...

A.   I've got my instructions

B.   what   bloody red-tape

A.   that I follow the regulations?

B.   if you had just a bloody little bit of good-will

	you wouldn't go on making a fool of your-self like this
A.	are you coming on or aren't you?
B.	were you born mean or have you been practising it for a long time?
A.	a new ticket or off you get
B.	dammit you ought to get a few basic lessons in ordinary human kindness and politeness
A.	I'll lose my temper in a second
B.	but of course I should be happy as a king because you're playing around with me like this
A.	I'm not taking any cheek from you
B.	but I'm to smile and take it I am
A.	off you get
B.	why don't you punch the ticket instead of making a row
A.	what ticket?
B.	right in front of your eyes does it have to be stuffed into your bake you're as blind as a bat
A.	you shut your bake now
B.	just imagine you are able to punch it
A.	I've got my regulations
B.	bloody hell what a democracy

EIGHTH SPEAKY

A.   do you mind if I move the bread?

B.   why should I?

A.   it's the paper you see
easier to read like this

B.   of course you just fix it for yourself

A.   it's nice to get a proper look at it

B.   of course you must have a proper look

A.   lord what a lot there is in the papers
I think

B.   you think so?

A.   yes I mean a lot of news

B.   news you think

A.   well of course you could say there's not so
much
depends on how you look at it

B.   of course you can look at it in different ways

A.   really in itself there's not much

B.   not much no

A.   strictly speaking there's really nothing

B.   just nothing at all

A.   not a bloody thing

though all sorts of things about what's
   happened
in it of course

B.   that's probably how it should be

A.   good lord there are people starving every-
               where
            in the world it says

B.   that's hardly news

A.   no of course but still
            I've heard that every second person or is
               it every third
            or every fourth or perhaps every fifth
               person
            is starving

B.   I've seen some figures
            about that somewhere too

A.   though it's only in those countries of course
            where there isn't any culture
            they haven't kept up with progress
            they've fallen behind

B.   I should think
            it's always like that
            some fall behind

A.   you'd think they could have noticed it in
               time

B.   noticed what

A.   that they've fallen behind

B.   people are conservative and blind like
               that
            can't see what it's all about
            till it's too late

46

A.   yes but isn't it bloody terrible all the same

B.   you could be right there

A.   you know sometimes you sort of wonder

B.   wonder did you say?

A.   yes about all this

B.   are you worried about it then?

A.   well shouldn't you
            shouldn't you worry about suffering?

B.   how should I know, does it make it any less?

A.   yes but they're suffering
            surely you can't get away from that anyway
            that they're suffering

B.   I've never met them

A.   but one surely ought to do something don't
              you think

B.   There are people who'll deal with it
            it's their job they're paid for it

A.   it's because there's so many of them of
              course

B.   oh it's because of that you think?

A.   well of course that's obvious dammit
            there wouldn't be so many suffering
            there wouldn't be so many hungry
            if there weren't so many
            that's as clear as daylight

B.   of course it's obvious there's a lot of them

A.   what can be done about it then

	that there's so many of them
B.	nothing not a bloody thing and then there'll be fewer of them of course
A.	but you just can't sit back and do nothing
B.	what sort of rubbish is that just as though we didn't have enough on our plate already
A.	dammit you know sometimes I'm afraid all the same
B.	afraid? what've you got to be afraid of?
A.	well you never know what could happen
B.	well is that anything to do with you
A.	no but all the same
B.	you shouldn't worry your heads so much about things people get what they deserve you know that
A.	no no don't tell me that
B.	what the hell's wrong with saying that
A.	it's not that dammit it's bloody Arsenal to think you can never rely on that damn team Bolton what sort of a shitty team's that?
B.	I haven't a clue about Bolton
A.	it's the dregs the absolute dregs

48

B.   oh come on now cheer up
            what about making some decision eh?
            what would you say to a steak?

A.   god yes I'm starving I could eat a horse

                    NINTH SPEAKY

A.   do you know what it is like to live?
            do you know what it is like every moment
            living so to speak next door to pain itself?

B.   of course of course I understand
            though naturally ...

A.   what's natural

B.   I mean it can be hard to really
            imagine what it's like

A.   because you don't want to yes
            because you're afraid to yes
            you don't really make a serious effort
                that's it

B.   oh but I do of course I do

A.   you know really it's strange
            what it's like to have an illness like this
            reveals people to you
            There's nothing tries another person more
            than just another person's suffering

B.   well indeed I suppose it tries the sufferer
                as well?

A.   perhaps
            wait a minute ohoh there there ah there
                now it's alright again
            wasn't so bad this time
            the small duct's not abducting you see

B.   ah you're able to laugh about it anyway

A.   my dear fellow one must one is forced to
            if life isn't to become completely intolerable
            you've got to be able to talk about what
                you're suffering from you know
            you've got to be able to live with your
                illness
            like an old friend

B.   ah yes of course

A.   you see this little indisposition I have
            musn't be confused with the atrophying
            of the heart muscles which is often ass-
                ociated with
            the more common acute infectious diseases
                you know
            I mean things like diptheria scarlet fever
            typhus pleurisy measles etc.

B.   no indeed I can see that

A.   now you know of course that atrophying
                can be hard
            to distinguish from the sort of
            heart disease which is caused by constric-
                tion in
            the main heart arteries you know the heart
                doesn't get
            enough blood
            and so atrophies little by little

B.   yes yes I see it can't get enough ...

A.   the only thing is that diseases like this
                affect
            every part of life
            you have to be careful about everything
            like now for example more than two or at
                most three
            whiskys is all I dare take
            same with food you know

50

at the most two or three courses for
  dinner
you've no idea what it's like
even when I go to the bog (john) I've got
  to be careful

B.   indeed it must be very trying

A.   you've no idea what it's like
          living under such a star of suffering
          it brands the whole of your life you know
          the least movement and breathlessness
            and palpitations
          feelings of terror and pressure in the chest
          you feel it in the whole of your body you see
          but worst of all's the terror you know
          it's as though someone with all his strength
          were holding it back with his thumbs

B.   that really must be rather unpleasant

A.   do you realize the pain?

B.   yes indeed I know I know

A.   It's real hell you know

B.   yes I know you know

A.   hell too that's just it
          that's just what you can never know you
            know
          you'd have to experience it yourself

B.   yes yes I know what you mean

A.   can you see it really demands spiritual
            strength
          if you're not to go under
          give up throw in the sponge

B.   no it can't be so easy to put up with no
            indeed

A.   it's not indeed it's not

B.   no indeed it isn't

A.   you can say that again

B.   you know I thought of asking you ...

A.   you seem very evasive

B.   not at all it was just something ...

A.   you thought the subject was unpleasant
          in some way?

B.   no no not at all it's not because of that at all

A.   don't you like to hear other people's
          suffering talked about?

B.   no no that hasn't anything to do with it

A.   perhaps you're trying to avoid facing up
          to life eh?

B.   no but my dear fellow it's not that at all
          it's only a thing I had

A.   are you completely insensitive to
          the suffering and difficulties of your
          fellow-men?

B.   good lord it was only something that con-
          cerned me
          I thought of mentioning something

A.   then you have really no interest in anything
          surely one should have a bit of sympathy
          at least?

B.   but yes of course one must have sympathy

A.   after all one must give a little of yourself

to others isn't that so
you shouldn't just evade the issue when
someone needs you

B.   it was only a thing I thought of asking you
about

A.   there's all too little sympathy in the world
that's the root of a lot of evil

B.   it's about a financial matter

A.   and maybe even of the
incurable isolation of human-beings my
friend

B.   it's a question of a little financial difficulty
really

A.   well of course people have financial
troubles
nothing to be surprised at with the irres-
ponsibility
that's so common nowadays but believe me
it's best not to get mixed up in it

B.   well I only thought of asking you if you
could possibly ...

A.   well of course I would
really would more than willingly
help people financially
but I don't on principle
It's only for the sake of the principle of the
thing you understand
and not because I don't want to help

B.   but it's not a question of a large ...

A.   sometimes one must sacrifice a little of
the personal
for the sake of the principle
even if it goes against the grain

B.	you know I'm in a spot of bother ...

A.	yes but my dear friend you shouldn't poke
	   you nose into
	other people's financial affairs
	quite simply it's none of your business
	it's good for people to learn
	to manage for themselves
	they must learn to manage for themselves
	   quite simply
	every human-being should stand on his own
	   two feet shouldn't he?
	it's every human-being's right to be allowed
	to sort out his own difficulties for himself
	without other human-beings pushing them-
	   selves in with their help

B.	yes certainly of course yes

A.	you must show a little simple human con-
	   sideration
	and not go blundering in with help and good
	   advice
	and anyway people shouldn't go round
	making their troubles public
	you should keep your troubles to yourself
	that's my motto

TENTH SPEAKY

A.	dear
B.	aye
A.	dear
B.	aye what's up now
A.	say something
B.	what do you mean say something

54

A.   surely you've got something to say

B.   shit

A.   you know quite well I meant
you should say something to me

B.   well hell that's not so bloody easy

A.   have you really got nothing at all to say
to me?

B.   what do you mean say to me?
there's millions of things to say

A.   so shit is the only thing you had to say to me
are you trying to say that I'm a shit
or don't I mean something more than a
shit to you?

B.   ah it's just that it's not so easy
to think of anything special to say

A.   no of course not
you had a million things to say
but you couldn't think of anything to say to
me nothing at all, no

B.   I was sitting thinking for god's sake

A.   oh I see it was because you were sitting
thinking
you hadn't anything to say

B.   you can't always think of something to say
there's nothing funny about that

A.   so you think it's too much for me to ask
that you speak to me just once just one
single time?

B.   I didn't say that

A.	do you think it's unfair of me to ask you for anything at all maybe?
B.	oh why must you go on like this now for?
A.	I'm not going on
B.	O.K. O.K. then we'll say you're not going on
A.	you said I was going on like this you said like what like this am I going on then?
B.	oh for god's sake you're just going on that's all
A.	like what like this I asked you
B.	don't you know yourself what you're behaving like?
A.	like what like this?
B.	like this dammit like you're behaving like dammit
A.	do you think that's any answer?
B.	answer, answer, dammit
A.	dear surely you shouldn't cut me off like that should you?
B.	no of course I shouldn't but what the hell
A.	you get so cross all over nothing
B.	but I'm not cross
A.	then everything's alright then you sounded so irritated you know
B.	you shouldn't keep thinking

about how I sound all the time

A.   then everything's alright then?

B.   of course it's alright

A.   then everything's really alright is it?

B.   certainly it's just as it should be

A.   dear how nice everything seems now doesn't
         it?

B.   certainly there's nothing wrong as far as
         I can see

A.   somehow it's just as it should be
         I think

B.   certainly it's just fine

A.   dear

B.   aye

A.   de-ear

B.   well what's up now

A.   are you in love with me?

B.   of course I'm in love with you

A.   but are you really in love with me?

B.   I said yes didn't I

A.   like really truly in love?

B.   well otherwise I wouldn't have said it

A.   yes but I mean really really in love?

B.   I love you dammit

A.   but why have you got angry like that again?

B.   I'm not
            angry I tell you

A.   if you really loved me
            you wouldn't shout at me like that

B.   but it's bloody well you that's shouting

A.   well that's no wonder
            the way you go on

B.   oh I'm the one that's going on now am I

A.   you're making a row like a railway station

B.   I'm making a row oh yes of course
            have you ever in your life heard that words
            are for thinking with
            and not just fill your gob with
            can't you think
            or is it just you don't want to?

A.   you musn't shout at me like that

B.   oh no but you must be allowed to talk
            any balls you like eh?

A.   oh what language you use

B.   thinking's beyond you
            is there anything you are capable of doing
               at all
            look what's this thing lying here for now
               then?
            and all this bloody mess here?

A.   I can't I just can't don't you see
            when you use that tone of voice to me

B.   just imagine you can never keep anything
                    in order
          can you do anything properly at all
          except blethering on

A.   you musn't talk to me like that
          you make me absolutely miserable can't
                    you see

B.   but sometimes you're completely impossible

A.   have you really nothing else to say to me?

B.   oh we're back there again are we

A.   there where's there?

ELEVENTH SPEAKY

A.   are you waiting for the last tram?

B.   yes I'm waiting yes
          and you?

A.   yes I'm waiting too

B.   oh

A.   it's late

B.   it's late yes

A.   but the evening's fine

B.   cloudless

A.   and yet full of warmth

B.   like a newly-opened hand

A.   or like a bed someone's just left

B.   yes

A.   how silent the city is

B.   it's not the city that's silent
             it's the people in it

A.   that's true

B.   yes

A.   I like waiting like this

B.   oh

A.   there's no-one to tell you off for waiting
             not even yourself

B.   that's true

A.   one can't do anything
             and one does it with a good conscience

B.   perhaps one is happy

A.   yes it could be one is

B.   in one way or another

A.   how silent the night is

B.   everything is silent
             it's only life that makes a row

A.   after all it's so eager

B.   for what?

A.   to live of course

B.   yes that's it

A.   here on earth

B.	a swinging green float riding on a swelling deep-blue sea
A.	yes maybe
B.	a glittering drop of warmth holding together
A.	the earth?
B.	no life
A.	ah life
B.	or the universe
A.	that's a fine image for our little warm nest in the world
B.	maybe so yes
A.	and there outside
B.	someone breathing on life's window
A.	loneliness?
B.	indeed certainly yes loneliness
A.	can you see the lights of the city? what beauty
B.	a shining loneliness
A.	and the rails look at the rails
B.	tracks to the stars
A.	they sparkle like a fever in the universe
B.	soon we won't see them anymore
A.	look can't you see that

                        the rails have no end

B.   yes indeed

A.   they lead from the street straight out
                            into the sky

B.   I can see it

A.   they haven't any end at all
                        they go straight to hell

B.   how could you know that

(The screen is now lowered over the stage again, it
says:

        ACT 3   PUBLIC SPEAKING

12 speaky on the screen inside a house)

                        TWELFTH SPEAKY

A.   come and look at this
                        it's something absolutely fantastic

B.   well what is it?

A.   read it darling
                        just read it

B.   no but it's really out of this world
                        it's absolutely fantastic

A.   isn't it just?

B.   yes but it's really wonderful

A.   lord lord one had hoped of course

B.   but that it should be a fact so quickly as
                            this
62

A.   can one be anything but happy?

B.   at last that's the phrase
at last it's here

A.   if I were a poet I'd write
an ode of triumph

B.   to think we should be allowed to experience
   this!

A.   what a happy day!

B.   the world suddenly seems quite new

A.   and life seems a better life

B.   it has meaning again

A.   like when the sun bursts out again after
long days of rain

B.   what one musn't forget on a day like this
is all the work that lies behind it
the gigantic human effort
which made this scientific feat possible

A.   and what a feat of science

B.   and what a moral feat
above all it is after all the human courage
behind it one admires

A.   courage yes that's it exactly yes
courage which carries humanity forward

B.   courage to go to the end
to draw the final conclusion

A.   yes exactly
to think as far as is possible

B.   not for one moment to try to bury

oneself in escapist reveries

A.   but to look reality in the face I mean

B.   that's it see it just as it is

A.   everything's like starting completely
                afresh

B.   at last you can breathe freely
                and consider the problem of life
                in a better way

A.   yes precisely yes

B.   at last war has become an impossibility
                with this humanity has arrived at the war
                to end all war
                with this there simply can't be any war
                for it comes to an end
                the very moment it starts

A.   how wonderful to know that

B.   there's an end of war now you know

A.   oh yes how wonderful

B.   there's an end to everything

A.   oh yes darling

B.   at last security is complete
                at last we master our future
                at last we control the whole of mankinds
                life or death

A.   just think

B.   doubt is blown away in one fell swoop

A.   oh yes and no-one needs to be uneasy

64

B.	no that's just it now fear is only stupidity and anxiety only lack of understanding of reality
A.	yes exactly there's no reason at all to be afraid in any way any longer
B.	now we can be happy instead
A.	glad and happy yes
B.	and brave and free like the men who freed the world from war who without fear or trembling perfected death
A.	oh dearest how glorious it still feels
B.	to think that it should still be like this it's like a fairy tale
A.	yes it's out of this world

(On the screen during the 13th speaky:

$$a = a$$
$$a = \text{not } b$$
$$a = \text{not } b \text{ or } c$$
$$a = \text{either } b \text{ or } c$$
$$\text{not } a = \text{not not } b$$

etc.)

THIRTEENTH SPEAKY

A.	have you thought of that?
B.	what?
A.	I said have you thought of that?

B.	and what might that be?
A.	what did you say?
B.	what might that be?
A.	are you asking me what that might be?
B.	are you asking me if I'm asking you what that might be?
A.	is it that you're asking me about?
B.	yes I'm asking you if you're asking me if I'm asking you what that might be
A.	what is it that might be
B.	might be?
A.	yes didn't you ask me what it is that might be?
B.	yes I was only wondering what it was that might be
A.	might be and might be there's very much that might be isn't there
B.	very much and very much what's very much?
A.	there's masses that's very much isn't there
B.	is there masses that's very much?
A.	yes it's quite obvious that there's masses that's very much
B.	it's obvious there's masses that's very much
A.	that's very possible

66

B.	well I'd hardly know anything about that
A.	well I didn't say that either
B.	whether you said it or not it has nothing whatsoever to do with the thing
A.	what's this you're talking about?
B.	am I talking about a thing? is there anyone who says that I'm talking about a thing?
A.	surely there's no-one saying anything about anything
B.	but what on earth's that got to do with the thing?
A.	what's this thing doing here again?
B.	ah stop harping on that thing now
C.	excuse me but I'd like to go back to what you were talking about at the start
A.	I didn't say anything at the start did I
B.	I don't understand at all what this has got to do with the thing
C.	it was a question of what you had thought surely, wasn't it?
A.	had I thought of something?
B.	but this is completely irrelevant in the context
C.	hadn't you thought of something?
A.	but wasn't it you who'd thought of something?

B.   why should it be just me
more than anyone else in the world who'd
    thought of something for?

C.   well I can hardly know what you'd been
    thinking for

A.   you've no right just to start expecting us
to know what you'd started thinking for

B.   but I don't at all
I've never thought I tell you

C.   I never asked you if you'd never thought
but if you'd thought <u>then</u>

A.   he asked you if you'd thought some other
    time?

B.   but I've never thought
then how could I be able to think I thought
some other time?

C.   a sharp-witted argument

A.   a weighty proposition

B.   yes isn't it?

C.   a convincing conclusion

A.   an exceptionally thoughtful hypothesis

B.   yes don't you think so?

C.   can you imagine a better-formulated
    problem?

A.   of such immense significance

B.   no indeed surely no-one can?

C.   but how should I be able to know that if
    anyone can?

68

A.   back again with one of these eternal
        questions again

B.   what are these eternal questions you're
        talking about?

C.   is he talking about questions?

A.   you've no right to go on expecting us
        to know the answers to everything

B.   but that's got nothing to do with the thing

C.   no but you really have no right to go on
        like that
    playing with your thing

A.   don't you realize there are masses of things
    which are more important than your little
        thing?

B.   but I don't care a bit about my thing

C.   I really don't know what one should say
        about that

A.   evasion of reality or exaggerated humility

B.   but I don't want to push my thing forward

C.   there's something strange about the whole
        thing I think

A.   something nastily hypocritical

B.   I don't give a fig for the thing I tell you

C.   almost an unhealthy odour about it all

A.   a perceptible spiritual deformation

B.   no but why must you keep going on like
        this for all the time?

69

C.   I don't quite understand your question

A.   no but now you really must stop
            asking like that

B.   like what

D.   I think it can really be absolutely fantastic

C.   when you say it
            it's obvious it can be

A.   strange that I hadn't thought of that earlier

B.   sounds very plausible

D.   yes indeed to think that ...

C.   what to think that?

A.   yes indeed what to think that

B.   yes then to think that what then?

D.   what to think that?

C.   you said to think that

A.   yes that's it, to think that you said

B.   your very words precisely that's it to
              think that you said

D.   oh what was I thinking of then?

C.   I can hardly know that

A.   he can hardly know that

B.   they can hardly know that either

D.   well what are you asking for then?

C. (to A. B.)   yes what are you asking that for?

A. (to B)   yes what are you asking that for?

B.   well I don't know what I was asking that
     for indeed I don't

D.   it's really unpleasant
     to ask me like that

C.   a nasty sort of curiosity

A.   to think you can never stop doing that

B.   well but what should one do to stop then?

D.   of course when you say that ...
     I mean one can

C.   yes indeed yes that's a different sort of way ...

A.   yes it's surely a question of whether ...

B.   yes to think that ...

D.   I don't know but

C.   so you mean that ...

A.   yes yes now I'm beginning to understand
     of course ...

B.   yes exactly the question is after all I
     mean ...

D.   what I mean is really well how should I put
     it ...

C.   I wonder if in fact ...

A.   well how do you think of ...

B.	it's as if well just how shall I put it ...
D.	oh well I'm not quite sure about that ...
C.	no but still it is surely a question of whether ...
A.	was it in some way or rather is it something ...
B.	it's as if well just how ...
D.	no I just thought of ...
C.	you mean one of those what's it called ...
A.	yes exactly one those they've got a term for it it's ...
B.	well I mean how one how shall I put it ...
D.	no well it was really nothing anyway ...
C.	yes of course it's obvious one could too as far as that goes ..
A.	yes of course I just don't understand
B.	what I mean is how ...
D.	yes that's just exactly what I mean
C.	but it really is immensely interesting
A.	a fascinating profound and scientific consideration
B.	I'm sorry but what that has got to do with the thing I can't see
D.	still it can't be helped that one in one way or another

must look at the whole question in the
   context
which the situation as a whole offers
even if one could undoubtedly imagine
the circumstances completely different

C.   it has been proved again and again that
one must commit oneself in principle to a
   thing
and then in practice do the opposite
still without there being in the thing as a
   whole
any change in the circumstances

A.   I find it hard to understand
why one therefore must throw out
the whole proposition even if the proposition
in reality has never been put forward

B.   no exactly

D.   I can't see that that is
anything but completely obvious

C.   we can positively assert that

A.   absolutely

B.   yes

(During the 14th speaky on the screen alternately
skulls, bony faces and hard determined faces. During
the song changes of colour)

FOURTEENTH SPEAKY

A.   now we'll have a talk about mankind

B.   yes indeed a few serious words

C.   a frank and open conversation

D.   about glorious humanity

A.   excepting individual human-beings of course

B.   yes children are bloody

C.   old people are disgusting

D.   women are horrible

A.   men are swine aren't they?

A. B. D. D.   yes the individual human-being is nix

B.   but humanity as such is the tops

C.   it is great

D.   it is a great rattling pile of bones

A.   crowned with its crown the cranium
                        the hard and rattling seed-pod

B.   with its 22 uplifted bones

C.   the lovely brain pan built of the paired
                        parietal bones, temporal bones, the unpaired
                        cervical bone, the sphenoid bone and the
                            ethnoid

D.   all the facial bones turned towards life
                        the outer paired nasal bones the super-
                            maxilliaries
                        the zygomatic bones the unpaired sub-
                            maxillary with the mental prominence
                        the chin the infra-orbital ridges the palatal
                            the lower nasal muscles and
                        the unpaired vomer besides the 32 teeth and
                        the three auditory bones

A.   the twelve pairs of long narrow flat and
                            curved ribs

74

B.   a wonderful residence for the governor
the heart

C.   fastened to his friend the spinal chord
populated by 24 free vertebrae, 7 cervical
  - 12 thoracic -
and 5 lumber vertebrae

D.   what an exemplary unity

A.   and the vertebra itself how wonderful the
    vertebra is, isn't it
with body and arch and transverse processes
the superior articular facet and the spinus
    process

B.   and the pelvic cavity the glorious door of
    our earliest home
through which we are pushed with shrieks
 and tumult

C.   and the pelvic built of its three paired bones
the ishial and illial and pubic bones and
the unpaired sacrum
the unity of the symphisis

D.   and the extremities with which we go to-
    wards others

A.   and with which we take from others

B.   with which we give to others

B.   with which we give to others
what we ourselves want rid of

D.   the arms with which we hold the one who
    wants to leave us

A.   or push away from us the one who wants to
    stay

B.   with the humerus and the forearms two bones

the olecrenon and the radius
the seven bones of the wrist besides the
little pissiform bone
the five bones of the metacarpus as well
as
the five fingers each one of them with
three bones
except the thumb which has two

C.   the legs with which we run from life
        and leave happiness behind us

D.   and which consist of the femur the lower
        leg with tibia and
        fibula tarsus metatarsus and toes which
        together build the foot

A.   the 4 lower bones of the tarsus form an
        arch
        the 3 upper are superior so in the tarsus
        itself
        there is only the spring ligament which
        rests on the
        posterior aspect of the calcaneum
        to which is attached the achilles tendon

B.   what a wonderfully constructed part of the
        world
        a working unity finer than co-operation

C.   bloody fine

D.   yes humanity and life are pretty hot stuff
        really

C.   Life you know

D.   eh?

C.   yes well life you know

B.   what?

C.   I'm going to explain this business about
               life

A.   oh I see this business about life

C.   well for God's sake don't look so damn
               sour about it

A.   who's looking sour then?

C.   well now keep quiet so I can explain life

A. B. D.   we're quiet as appendices

C.   well then life I'm going to explain life
               life my friends life that is
               now then let us look at life now

A.   now?

C.   you musn't interrupt me like that
               now I've completely lost the thread of
                  what I was going to say
               damn I had it just on the tip of my tongue
                  too

B.   well we could hardly know you had it just
               there

A.   my dear friends I think the explanation is
               very simple
               one should quite simply live life properly

B.   yes exactly I think so too one should
               live life properly

C.   properly yes exactly

D.   properly yes that's very probable

A.   it's obvious one should live it properly

D.   how properly

A.	well surely you understand that properly I mean properly properly without any fancy business
D.	actually I think it's even simpler quite simply I think the purpose of life is that one should be happy
B.	yes of course how could I be so silly
C.	it's quite obvious when you say it it's happiness one should have
A.	it's easy to say that but how do you get happiness?
D.	eating good food and being able to do what you want that's happiness in life
A. B. C.	yes of course
A.	but look humanity then?
D.	well what about it then?
A.	that's just it what about it then?
D.	well surely there's nothing wrong with it?
A.	yes but we were going to talk about humanity we should explain it as well
D.	surely there's nothing to explain
B.	yes but what's its purpose
D.	the purpose of humanity is to be old the older the better
C.	ah ha it should grow old

78

D.   yes that's its purpose

C.   and grow happy

D.   the older the happier

A. B. C.   it's wonderful to know that

A.   that happiness is waiting for us

A. B. C. D. (SONG without stop, accompanied)

when Jones has grown old
and stopped masturbating
then Smith has grown ancient
and starts talking balls
and sergeant Ryan dodders
and gets tired and ratty
just like little miss Andersson
who decays in her shop
and Hector in the pulpit
grows old in the meantime
and loses all his hair
and young mr Chambers
goes rancid like butter
and couldn't give a fart
while missus Johnson
goes sour beneath her breasts
and Eric Trim gets heavy
and crawls up the stairs
and lovely little Alice
grows fat as a walrus
and stupid as a haddock
while Brian in his house
shits his guts asunder
while the years blow on
like a snowstorm on his skull
and Martin the builder
couldn't raise a laugh two inches
and little miss Abrahams
falls to pieces in the gut
and stops dreaming of a fuck
in the meantime Alfred ages

in his heavy, straying wits
and begins to go deaf
and can't see much
and begins to smell badly
something really bloody awful
and stupid podgy Andrew
can't move an inch
and can't dammit remember
what his name was yesterday
and there's a squeaking gurgle
from old Wilson the maths. teacher
like a rusty old waterpipe
and old Pearson the conductor
and nice sister Armstrong
and the reverend Grummage and
Bill Bloggins the foreman
have crumpled up to
small dry and bony fruits
Oh then old Peter's sitting
with no teeth and is so happy
like all the old who've grown old
because he's grown old
and that'd given meaning to his life
O then old Hilda limps
on her only crooked leg
grey and snivelling with age
happy as a grey seal in its sea
while pain screams like a fog-horn
through her mist-marooned body
and professor Thomas Greenwood
sits with constipation
and stomach-ache without end
a happy old heap of bones
for the rest of his life
O the aged human-being
groaning as he walks
feeling death beneath his fingers
full of holes like a wicker-gate
broken like a ragged fence
and old as a heath
but happy and glad
so he nearly can't contain himself
O the aged human-being

80

bent over his back and
decrepit as a windmill
but glad as Christmas pud
and happy as an Irish stew
how happy is the human-being
when he flickers like a candle
hardly human and with only
one finger still in life
oh but happiest of all
when he finally stops living.

(During the 15th speaky the speaker in a spotlight,
screen red. Perhaps echo effect towards the end)

FIFTEENTH SPEAKY

Stop there blast you don't try to slip away
oh yes don't say anything you knew quite well
I wanted to speak seriously to you
are you afraid of seriousness perhaps?
Oh certainly it's in harmony with the
    spirit of the times after all
everyone does what you tried to do
slip away and bury their head in the sand
It just won't do, don't you realize that?
The world expects every man to do his
    duty
attack the evil in the world
What are you doing for example to prevent
the spread of atomic weapons?
Have you prevented one little small atom
    bomb perhaps?
Oh yes don't start making excuses for
    yourself
isn't it every human-being's duty to do that?
I mean prevent bombs, well isn't it?
No, no it's better for you to keep quiet
now you can't try to dodge the issue
it's a question of your contribution
that others do less than you
is that any excuse for you to do less than
    them?

O.K. you yourself haven't invented any bomb
that's quite possible
that's how it should be
but that you haven't got rid of one single one
is I must say worse
You admit then that you do nothing
and don't want to do anything?
Your silence is really serious
are you a thinking human-being?
then think damn you
have you thought of the population explosion?
What are you doing to prevent the increase
    of children?
O.K. it's possible that you haven't yourself
produced any children
that's how it should be
but that you haven't got rid of one single one
is really disgusting
haven't you the slightest sense of respon-
    sibility?

(On the screen, summer-house in the garden.
At the beginning of the conversation petulant whispers
murmurings, groans and gasps over the loudspeaker
Gradually the sound increases, at the end the speakers
shout with their heads close together over the table)

SIXTEENTH SPEAKY

A.   there's no tea-pot

B.   you're right
            do you think she can have forgotten it?

C.   (in with a tea-pot places it with a little
            bang on the table. Then puts a rich and
            heavily brocaded tea-cosy over the pot)

B.   I can't stand things like that

A.   don't you like tea-cosies?

B.   I get quite sick as soon as I even see a tea-cosy

C.   mother made it
                   she was very good at sewing

B.   oh I'm sorry I'm afraid I'd forgotten that completely

D.   perhaps you meant that you didn't mean that you
                   didn't like just that particular tea-cosy
                   but only felt ill from tea-cosies in general?

A.   personally I like tea-cosies very much

D.   a proper tea-cosy is a very worthwhile thing I think
                   a proper tea-cosy is in my opinion
                   a tea-cosy that works

C.   would anyone like some tea?

B.   no thank you it doesn't agree with me

D.   not for me thank you

A.   I'll give it a miss too if I may thank you all the same

C.   then I won't bother bringing in the water for the tea

A.   you must admit that it's restful to sit here with a cup of tea in perfect peace

B.   yes indeed one needs to relax with a cup of tea

D.   I think that a proper cup of tea properly used
                   can change people

C.   I made it the way mother did

B.   of course I'm afraid I'd forgotten that
            do give me a cup please

A.   sitting here forgetting all the troubles of
              the world

B.   and having a rest from all that talk
            about all the people in misery in the world

D.   how nice it is

B.   on the other hand it's really all that misery
            that makes one put all the more value
            on one's own good life

D.   obviously

A.   yes indeed there is no better spice for food
            than the thought of all the hungry now is
              there?

C.   perhaps I can offer you a little marzipan
              cake?

B.   please that would be delightful

D.   I certainly can't resist that

A.   I'd say please immediately

C.   it's made from mothers recipe

B.   yes of course yes I'd forgotten that
            could I have two bits please

A.   really glorious sitting here
            with one's little bit of cake

B.   an exceptional gateau I must say

D.   in my opinion marzipan cake
            is something that should be used

84

C.   mother always offered guests marzipan
                 cake

B.   oh I say I'd completely forgotten that

A.   besides I don't think one should believe
                 too much
           of all that talk about everything

B.   the papers distort so much and make it up
           and make everything more terrible than
                 it is

A.   there's such an immense number of happy
                 people
           though one never hears anything about them

D.   the real state of affairs is
           that practically speaking every human-
                 being
           is happy in some way
           one shouldn't forget that

B.   if one is to be fair yes

C. (to A)   did you hear that?
           mother always used to offer marzipan cake
                 to her guests

A.   fantastic I really hadn't an inkling of that

C.   no but actually she did

A.   just think

D.   I'm sorry what was it we should think

C.   well I just said it
           my mother always used to offer marzipan
                 cake to her guests

D.   really I didn't know that at all

C.   no but actually that's just what she did

D.   just imagine

A.   how upset people can get over nothing at all

B.   people yes it's quite fantastic

A.   like this business with the two-and-a-half
                    -year old boy who
          was found dead among his toys on the
                    kitchen floor

B.   yes of course yes it was the kitchen floor

A.   his step-father had lost his temper because
                    the boy cried
          when the wife went to work
          and he wanted to sleep

B.   yes of course yes he wanted to sleep

D.   I think his anger should be seen
          as a completely natural reaction
          since he probably hadn't slept during the
                    night

B.   of course one loses one's temper if you
                    can't sleep

A.   but that the child hadn't the sense to keep
                    quiet all the same

D.   the probability is that the mother stopped
                    the father
          from sleeping during the night
          and therefore strictly speaking is res-
                    ponsible for what happened

B.   one knows what women are like
          nagging and nagging so you get water on
                    the knee

C.   you know quite well that mother never
       nagged

B.   I'm sorry I didn't think of that

C.   wasn't it terribly irresponsible of the
       mother to go
    off just like that
    surely a mother should after all first and
       foremost
    think of her little child?

B.   besides such a small child doesn't suffer
       at all

A.   of course not

B.   old people whose life one takes maybe

A.   I agree

B.   but someone so young

A.   yes of course

B.   hardly knew what happened

A.   such a small child doesn't know what fear is

B.   why make a fuss about it?

C.   well did he get to sleep afterwards?

B.   well naturally you can see that
    when the child died he was quiet of course

C.   of course it's obvious he was quiet

A.   yes it's just continual complaining
    about one thing or another

B.   and completely unnecessary

D.   can anyone understand what people really
                   want?
          like the teachers who complain
          about there being children in the schools

A.   or all the old people who go around com-
                   plaining
          about anything and everything

D.   strictly speaking old people have no needs
          and therefore nothing to complain about

A.   should people who have life
          and therefore all their troubles
          behind them go round making a fuss?

B.   and it's so boring too to sit
          and listen to how much they suffer

C.   yes just think how mother complained and
                   she certainly suffered

B.   oh yes of course I'd completely forgotten
                   that

D.   it's so ugly too to have all the old people
                   suffering
          pain is the private business of every sufferer
          but everyone is tormented by its unpleasant
                   apearance, isn't that so?

C.   people ought to stay indoors when
          they're suffering they really ought

A.   ah well it's wonderful anyway

B.   sitting here like this yes
          and leaving other people to their own devices

D.   leaving?

B.   are we going to leave?

D.		I thought you said we were leaving
C.		Oh no don't go do sit a bit longer do there's more of the cake
A.		what did you say?
C.		cake
A.	(to B. D.)	just a moment have you seen the cake?
C.		no no the cake's here
A.		what are you asking for the cake for if you know where it is?
C.		I didn't ask where it was I only said there was some more of it
A.		yes yes I think so too
B.		what was that?
A.		I think so too
B.		naturally
D.		the main thing is that we're having a nice time
B.		sorry what did you say?
D.		a nice time
B.		great to get a bit of peace and quiet and silence yes
A.		what did you say?
B.		what?
A.		I said what did you say?

B.   did you hear what he said?

D.   hear what?

B.   haven't a clue

A.   anyway we're having some peace and quiet
                  I said we're having some peace and quiet

B.   who's got what did you say?

C.   well I only meant that there was more of
                     the
                  cake that is
                  I said the cake
                  the cake

(After the 16th speaky sign lowered over the stage
again, on it:

               ACT 4 OUR WORLD AND US

On the stage during the 17th speaky
a woman in strong light
a man hardly visible
the rest darkness)

               SEVENTEENTH SPEAKY

          death oh did you say that did you say that,
               death, did you?
          isn't it a wonderful word death?
          there's no more beautiful word anywhere,
               dearest
          maybe the word star the word STAR
          is as beautiful nearly as beautiful
          it must be because all the stars are dead
          that the word is so beautiful
          don't you think that's it?
          Oh I like you so much I'd
          like to bury you do you know that

with lots of wonderful flowers darling
masses whole mountains of flowers darling
death of yes let us talk more about death
  darling
there's nothing more wonderful than that
how beautiful it is
everything that's past
there's nothing more wonderful than
dead people
don't you think so darling?
idiot you musn't look like that
you know quite well I love
you when you're alive as well
I mean it's so wonderful to have you here
  dearest
oh you're my little sweetie
my peach my piggy my lollipop
the dearest dearest drummer of my heart
you know I think love is the
nearest death one can come
that's why love is so wonderful isn't it
that's why everyone wants to die
when they're in love, don't you think so?
you know I don't think people
would love each other if there weren't death
my dearest darling
don't you think so too?
I mean that life gets its value
only through death
gets its meaning its depth its brilliance
yes everything that makes it worth living
only through death?
no you don't need to say anything my dear
I see in your eyes the answer
Oh how wonderful it is to agree
it's nearly like being dead don't you think
  so?
dearest, isn't it strange
that people can be afraid of death
or dislike it
death is after all the limitless
in death there's every possiblity
death is a promise that never fails

don't you think so too?
lord as for life
there's only one possibility to live isn't
   there?
life my darling is a promise
that is never fulfilled
it's hardly anything to think so marvellous
   is it
you know isn't it too too wonderful
with really old people
it's as though one could feel
death when one touches them
old people are so awfully happy too
have you noticed that?
it's just because they as it were
walk hand in hand with death
and soon will be dead and really happy
Oh how I love the dead
dearest when all the living are dead
then you can see they only wanted the best
   can't you
yes yes I know what you want to say
that you can't understand how anyone can
   grieve
when someone goes and dies
it's us really who should grieve
who should grieve because we're not dead
   already
don't you think so?
die Oh yes if I could die how nice it must
   be to die
Oh if only I could die over and over again
my darling

(During the 18th speaky sky at night with stars on the
screen.
The pillar is a book case)

EIGHTEENTH SPEAKY

A.   look here old man would you be very
                     annoyed

	if we asked you to read some of your poems now?
B.	Oh yes that would be wonderful
C.	no no not at all of course I'd be delighted of course
B.	poetry's so marvellous and so instructive
C.	well I don't quite know if it's instructive
B.	oh but yes yes indeed it is it is do you know it's poetry that taught me how to live in a beautiful and true way
C.	I don't quite know what to say
A.	there's something illuminating about good poetry
C.	well perhaps there is
A.	would you like candle light to read by?
C.	oh it's fine without it
A.	oh yes candle light creates such a wonderful atmosphere
D.	it makes it easier to concentrate on the poetry
C.	oh well then
A.	is that O.K. or maybe you'd like a different one or another one as well or shall I put it on the other side?
C.	thanks thanks that's just fine

A.   maybe I should get a cushion?

C.   really it's fine as it is

A.   well then now we must be quiet so that the
                poetry can be heard

B.   oh yes read lots and lots

A.   just wait a second
            I'll dash out and get some chocolates
            I think we should give ourselves a real
                treat
            and let both body
            and soul   enjoy the best shouldn't we?

C.   well you really think of everything

D.   certainly you should spoil yourself
            and enjoy life sometimes

A.   can you all reach the chocolates now?
            are you all comfortable now?
            no-one's got the light in their eyes?
            then we'll be absolutely quiet
            quiet as mice blinded by the light of poetry

B.   oh how nicely put

A.   ssh now we're all ears

C.   I'll read from my last collection
            "Words instead"

A.   I'm sorry but we will hear some of the
                little poems
            from the other books as well won't we?

D.   your last book is certainly a monumental
                work
            no-one could deny that
            but still I think it oughtn't to overshadow
            all your earlier stuff

94

A.   right then quiet now and let the magic of
        poetry
        exert all its power

C.   I'll start then

B.   isn't it wonderful now?

A.   quiet now and let our poet read

B.   oh I'm sorry it's just so wonderful
        to really feel all of us that it's wonderful
        it is wonderful isn't it?

D.   I think you could say it gives a really
        extraordinarily fine sense of community
        besides what's poetry for really when it
          comes down to it
        except just a sense of community?

C.   then I'll begin with the first poem in the
          collection
        the poems have no titles
        so I'll make a little pause between them

D.   oh sort of commoners are they then?

A.   no now you really must be quiet
        or our poet will never be able to read

B.   oh yes do start
        I'm so awfully impatient

A.   if only you knew how happy I am
        I've really been looking forward to this

C.   then I'll start then
        'There's a boom when the nut-case strikes ... '

A.   oh oh just a second
        you won't be angry will you if we interrupt
          you?
        I mean if we want to ask you about something
          or other?

C.   of course not
        it's just grand if you ask questions

B.   what a fine attitude to people you have
        I think

C.   then I'll begin again then
        well I'll start from the beginning since
        I had only read one line
        'There's a boom when the nut-case strikes ...'

A.   oh look I am sorry but just a second
        do you want us to ask questions in between
          the poems
        when you make that little pause you talked
          about
        or can we interrupt you in the middle
        I mean just when anyone thinks of it
        I mean when we want to ask?

C.   my dear fellow please naturally you can
        interrupt me just when you like

A.   yes that's all I wanted to know
        you know you can hurt someone so easily
        just through pure ignorance

C.   right then I'll begin at the beginning
          again then
        'There's a boom when the nut-case strikes ...

B.   but that's just wonderful

A.   an extraordinarily good beginning really
          I must say

D.   what a powerful attack
        that's just the sign of great poetry
        that it reveals its greatness from the very
          first line

C.   I'm glad you like it

D.	like's hardly the right word

C.	well shall I go on with the rest now

A.	of course we want to hear it all

C.	I'll begin with the first line it'll be easier to read the poem then 'There's a boom when the nut-case strikes ...'

A.	I'm sorry but I think that that line is really exciting it says far more than one imagines at first sight

B.	oh yes doesn't it

D.	indeed it does

A.	but it's not what you'd call easy to under- stand is it I mean like Wordsworth and all that

B.	sometimes you can't understand at all what these modern poets mean

C.	but the best thing about modern poetry is
	  surely just that
	that you really must appropriate it for
	  yourself
	that you yourself in a sense give the poem
	  its meaning

A.	but can you really expect that of people of an ordinary simple man? isn't it the poets job to write the poem so that the ordinary simple man can understand it? sometimes I wonder if there isn't something undemocratic about expecting something like that in a way?

D.	the line is I think extremely expressive

so it isn't that at all
but isn't there a little contempt in it
I mean isn't there an indifference
a feeling of superiority over just the
ordinary simple man in the line?

B.   yes I think the line expresses
a terribly negative attitude to life

C.   it really depends a bit on how you read
the poem

B.   but still nut-case surely can't be anything
positive
to say about a human-being can it?

C.   but after all one must think of the context
the word is in
I mean the context of the whole poem

B.   but we're talking about the first line now
aren't we?

C.   yes yes but I mean

B.   anyway I'm talking about the first line

C.   well of course we're talking about the
first line

B.   well there you are

D.   I'm just thinking of that contemptuousness
in the poem
is it really something positive to be
contemptuous do you think?
for after all it is something positive that
the poem wants to and must give isn't it?

C.   it's not so easy to answer that
I mean one does want to be honest as well

A.   well isn't there anything positive in life
then?

98

C.   but of course there are positive things in
                         life

A.   well there you are then

B.   what I can't understand is how a poet
                         can be bothered to go on with something
                            where
                         there's no meaning at all

C.   but my dear friend of course
                         it doesn't seem meaningless to write poetry

B.   but you said a minute ago that what the
                         poet wrote
                         had no meaning in it
                         it was up to us the readers to make
                         a meaning of it or something like that

A.   I don't know but I think you're so undem-
                         ocratic
                         when you mean something in a poem like
                         that
                         surely it's still the reader who has the
                         right to decide
                         what the poem says hasn't he?

D.   there's an isolation from life in the whole
                         poem
                         an aristocratic judgment on people
                         and by the way why have you got candles?
                         don't you believe in your own poetry
                         do you have to use conjuring tricks?

C.   but I never asked for candles

D.   if you'd said no you'd not have had candles

C.   but what could I do ...

D.   are you trying to tell us that we forced
                         candles on you?

C.   no of course you didn't

D.   very well then

B.   someone was talking about undemocratic
                     and so on
is it really right to write a poem
which is full of contempt for the reader
and all humanity
I mean isn't it the right of human-beings
to be able to read about the beautiful
                     things in life
isn't it the duty of the poet in his poetry
to communicate the beauty that exists?

D.   undemocratic and undemocratic
I think there's something unbearably pre-
                     tentious
and authoritarian in forcing on people in
                     the poem like this
everything that's ugly and nasty

B.   do you really think you should behave like
                     that?

D.   in a way it strikes me
as unparalleled egotism

A.   anyway what right have you really to write
                     poems
and palm your experiences off on us

C.   I don't understand at all
no-one's trying to palm off on you
have you ever come across a poet who
                     palmed off anything
have I palmed off in any way?

A.   dear dear you are touchy
I never said you palmed off

D.   no-one here said you palmed off

A.   surely you won't assert that one of us
has accused you of palming anything

100

if you do it is most unjust
and not like you at all

C.   no for god's sake
        I haven't said
        that one of you said
        that I palmed

A.   well O.K. then
        then you've no need at all to lose your
           temper

D.   we're only too willing to ask you to forgive
           us
        if you've misunderstood us in some way

A.   now come on don't be so cross any longer
        it's nothing to get het up about
        not one of us thinks
        you palmed anything off in any way

D.   no it's surely nothing to fight about

A.   you know very well that we love your poetry

B.   oh do read it again won't you?

D.   we're really dying to hear the rest

B.   start again from the beginning with that line
        'there's a bang'

C.   'boom'

B.   oh yes 'boom'
        the line 'there's a boom when when when ...'

C.   'the nut-case'

B.   oh yes 'nut-case' that's it
        'there's a boom when the nut-case nut-
           case nut-case nut- ...

C.   'strikes'

B.   yes that's how it went of course
                    'there's a boom when the nut-case strikes'
                    do start at that line again won't you?

(The 19th speaky is spoken by a man with a pipe in a
dressing-gown he has a book on his knee.
During the pauses there are pictures of soldiers
marching to loud military music on the screen, as
he speaks the screen and the pillar are a beautiful
green)

                    NINETEENTH SPEAKY

                first and foremost I want to make it
                    absolutely clear
                that I certainly do not want to suggest
                that war is desirable
                no no certainly not
                war is and always will be
                something that goes against humanity
                isn't that so
                but I say but
                and I stand by that
                one must be positive
                and judge everything in the best possible
                    light
                shouldn't one
                it's quite obvious that one can think
                that war has its unpleasant aspects
                I'm not saying anything about that
                after all that has a completely natural
                    explanation
                but one must not neglect the positive side
                if one wants to be just to war
                is there anything so democratic as war?
                in the face of death we are all free
                we are all equals and brothers
                since we are all going to die
                why not do it together and at the same time?
                you know there's something else here as
                    well

it is after all a fact that high consumption
is our civic duty
for the maintenance of our welfare
well then what about cannons tanks and
   bullets
who eats bullets?
war
war eats cannons tanks and bullets
we need war
so that our weapons can be consumed
and our welfare maintained
without war our production would be held
   up
and consequently the whole rise in our
   standard of living
that really isn't difficult to figure out
but of course that isn't to say that war
has not got its negative aspects
one must after all be just
and not overlook the fact
that war can also have its darker side
we all know that human-beings die because
   of war
and that is obviously not
always very pleasant
on the other hand we ought not to forget
that people must die because of it
this is after all the basic idea of war
that's something one cannot avoid
now I'm not saying that human-beings
   ought to die
I'm only saying that if one has war
then people must die because of it
after all otherwise it wouldn't be a war
   at all
after all there's no use going on with a war
and afterwards pretending it was a butter-
   fly chase
now is there?
I mean once one really has made the
   decision
to kill people
then it's a matter of killing as many as
   possible

and then it must be wrong
if just through carelessness or lack of
  thought
one didn't manage to kill more than perhaps
a fraction of the number one with a little
  better
planning and consideration could have
  killed
is that not so?
now I want to say immediately that I
can very well understand
the people who feel a little uncertainty
  about the atom bomb
it is obvious that that causes a not incon-
  siderable amount
of disorder when it is used
but on the other hand it has an effectiveness
which really cannot be forgotten
and looked at from the point of view of war
is indeed an eminently useful thing
if one has really studied the thing
it means a fine step forward
as far as I can see, it is
isn't it a crime against the idea of war
not to use the atom bomb
now it's quite obvious that someone can
  object
and there is probably something in it
that there just won't be any human-beings
  left
if over-much use were made of it
it's quite obvious that for the survivors
there must be a certain amount of trouble
but for the dead after all all troubles are
  out of the world
and good lord if there were
no survivors
there'd be no-one at all to grieve
and all troubles would be out of the world
and so I don't quite understand
what one has to complain about, do you?
besides war and war
why talk about war all the time

when in most cases its
a question of a completely peaceful action
merely carried on by violent means?

(After the 19th speaky, darkness, in the darkness a
chill gust of wind. During the 20th speaky the profiles
of the speakers seen on the white screen)

TWENTIETH SPEAKY

A.   dad

B.   yes my boy

A.   I can't help it
            sometimes I wonder all the same

B.   well wonder what son

A.   no anyway it's nothing really

B.   no no come on just say what you mean

A.   ah I don't know

B.   don't be afraid
            just you tell me what you were worrying
              about

A.   you know dad
            I can't help it
            but sometimes I wonder all the same
            dad how could you do that to me?

B.   what do you mean do what to you?

A.   ah don't play around
            you know quite well what I mean

B.   are you going to drag up that old story
              again?

A.   dad I asked you
            how could you do that to me?

B.   ach well

A.   but dad I hung so uncomfortably

B.   yes yes I know

A.   it ached

B.   ached did it

B.   just think how much it ached
            ached and burned and stung
            and I couldn't see a thing with the blood
              in my eyes

B.   yes yes of course I'm sorry
            you had such a bad time my boy
            but still you must try to forgive me

A.   forgive forgive it's not that
            I just don't understand what I was meant
              to be doing
            up on that damned cross

B.   you musn't say that

A.   but what did you mean by it
            what did you mean by the whole thing
              anyway

B.   well I meant ...
            well I meant something ...

A.   something what's something?

B.   it's not so easy to remember now
            it's so long ago

A.   but you meant something anyway?

B.   I meant well ...
            yes that's what I meant
            I meant well

A.   you abandoned me that's what you did
            you wanted rid of me that's what it was

B.   but my dear boy

A.   this resurrection was something you hadn't
               counted on, eh?

B.   but why are you taking it all like that?
            of course you know I didn't mean it that
               way

A.   if you'd really liked me
            you'd never have done it and that's that

B.   but heavenly mother what on earth do you
               mean?
            of course I loved you son
            I love you absolutely immensely
            I tell you
            you're the only one I have aren't you?

A.   that's just why I don't get it
            can't you understand I suffered
            I had a bloody awful time of it

B.   oh well I suffered too let me tell you
            really it's quite possible that I suffered
               more

A.   in theory maybe
            but I suffered in practice
            damn me that was more immediate I can
               tell you
            I got good and sick of it

B.   well now now don't get all upset unecc-
               arily my boy
            dammit I've said I'm sorry haven't I

A.   that doesn't make any difference it was you
        arranged the whole miserable business for
          me
        you're the one who's responsible for it

B.   you're just like all the others
        accusing me of everything
        everything's my fault
        never a thank you or a good word
        everyone blames me
        when there's something wrong with them
        but what about me
        can I help that I am what I am
        can I do things differently from what I do
        well can I?

A.   all the same if you'd wanted to
        you could have done something completely
          different

B.   but for heaven's sake boy
        it's not just a question of what I want
        it's much more complicated that that

A.   O.K. then let's not talk about it any more

B.   what's up with you anyway?
        it isn't all that bloody easy for me all the
          time
        I can tell you

A.   we won't talk about it any more I said
        the matter's finished
        I guess you had your way

B.   ah now don't start again
        you really must in all seriousness under-
          stand
        that I can have my own big problems too
        I just don't know where people get the
          idea from
        that I should be able to manage everything
        things can get a bit mixed up now and again
          I can tell you

108

A.   yes but there ought to be some limit to
                the mess

B.   but dammit it was the first time after all
                that's not so easy

A.   the first time?

B.   yes the first time what's wrong with that?

A.   no you don't mean that I'm going down
                there again?

B.   now now don't get all excited again

A.   don't you realize it'll be
                ten times worse this time?
                they've had practice
                they've got new technical resources
                I haven't a chance
                it would be hell can't you see that?

B.   we'll talk about it some other time
                when you're not so upset my son

A.   it's the same thing every time
                evasions and excuses
                to kingdom come

B.   there there my son my boy
                you musn't forget how much
                your old father loves you

A.   yes yes it's just as it should be I suppose
                why on earth should anyone care about me?
                that's probably why I exist of course
                to be a sort of door-mat in front of para-
                    dise
                for them to wipe their sinful boots on

B.   well what kind of a way
                is that to talk about Jesus

(After the 20th speaky, sign down over the stage
again:

ACT 5 WAGES OF FEAR)

TWENTY-FIRST SPEAKY

A.   please please
     Oh won't you listen to me for a few
      moments
     oh just a few moments a very few will you?

B.   naturally I am very willing to be of any
      help I can
     perhaps you have some problem
     which you need to discuss with some im-
      partial person

A.   oh how could you know that?
     indeed I have a problem
     dear lord my great problem is loneliness
     I haven't a single human-being I can be with
     You get so tired of just sleeping
     you get so sick of just eating
     just working is so miserable

B.   of course you don't have to be
     so lonely and not have friends and acquain-
      tances
     at your age you ought not and must not
     think life is frankly miserable
     The town you live in ought surely to be
     full of human-beings isn't it?

A.   where I work there are lots of
     married women and young girls but
     there's no unmarried girl-friend for me
     there's no-one to go around with for me
     there's no-one at all
     it makes me so miserable

B.   my dear it is a duty
for a young person like you to be happy
Go and invite some people from work home
for a real party
you'll see that they'll all come
and have great fun with each other
and just imagine how nice it will be for you
to see and hear their happiness

A.   oh but don't you understand that
I don't know how to get into contact with
    people
I just about blush when I say my name
don't you understand
I don't dance
I don't belong to clubs
I don't like making conversation
and I get awful feelings of fear
when I'm sitting in the cinema

B.   my dear one just must not be unhappy at
    your age
Can you be too shy and reserved perhaps?
Perhaps a little drive
and initiative from you
wouldn't be a bad idea?
If any of the people at work need a baby-
    sitter some evening
surely you could offer your services?
you can do what you want with
children if they are small enough of course
and actually there is a lot one can do with
    children
if one has a little imagination and invent-
    iveness

A.   yes yes I do understand
but I really want so much to meet a man
It is just that it isn't so easy to get
hold of a man
since I never meet one
Heavens I don't know at all
what is it one says to one?

I don't know at all
what is it one does with one?

B.   one must not at your age be so lonely
          absolutely not
        at least you must realize
        there are after all so many interests you
        can develop
        different sorts of courses for example

A.   but don't you understand
        how can you have
        interests when you are as lonely as I am?
        I've hardly got the energy to live
        so how can I have the energy to be inter-
          ested in anything else?
        Every year I've advertised
        for a girl-friend without any result
        'Are you the friend I sought for everywhere?'
        Reply to sad and lonely'
        But it's only men that answer
        and I don't know at all what one
        answers a man
        oh my dear dear friend
        I hardly know what one answers at all

B.   no matter what the circumstances you
          must and shall at your
        age from now on stop being so miserable
          and depressed
        What about improving
        your knowledge of languages?
        Perhaps people do not understand what
          you say?
        Perhaps you do not speak the language
        spoken around you?

A.   sometimes I'm completely sick
        completely sick from loneliness do you
          understand
        I'm absolutely too lonely
        to bear being lonely
        I'm so outside of things

and I can't see anyone at all there inside
there's no-one at all around
please please help there are limits to what
  one can take
and soon I won't be able to take any more

B.   my dear someone as young as you are must
not be so desperate my dear
you do understand that you must not don't
  you
I sincerely hope that your
situation will improve
and that you find the companionship you
  long for
If you do not succeed
you must certainly try to live a different
  life
a life like everyone else's
where you will not need to be so lonely
  will you?

(During the 22nd speaky when children are mentioned,
pictures of children on the screen, e.g. bits of
film giving the impression of children streaming
forward.
Perhaps some of the sections about children can be
recited)

TWENTY-SECOND SPEAKY

A.   what is it making that noise?

B.   nothing in particular
it's life going on
people happy with each other

C.   happy?

B.   yes someone tortures another and it makes
  him happy

A.	it sounds unpleasant it's rather nasty to listen to it
B.	but still at least one person is gloriously happy aren't they?
A.	I hadn't thought of that
B.	no we are indeed blind to the sources of happiness in life
C.	that puts a different light on the thing of course
A.	I don't know but there's something strange
D.	there's something that isn't right
B.	well what's up now?
A.	there's something in the air
B.	you think there's a smell?
A.	yes isn't there a sort of smell doesn't it smell bad?
D.	death perhaps that smells or love that has a smell too anyway there is a smell
B.	good lord everything that's alive smells after all
D.	it smells as if I were inside the clothes of dirty life itself
C.	ugh what an imagination you have
D.	but I think it's horrible it's like a hospital smell or as if death had chanced to uncover himself

114

B.	you'll see there's always a breeze comes and it disappears anyway the more it smells the less you smell it
D.	I hadn't thought of that
B.	you can't think of everything
A.	but still it's strange all the same
B.	ah yes
A.	isn't it getting darker
C.	yes isn't it getting darker
B.	of course it's getting dark
A.	just as I thought
B.	yes
C.	I'm afraid
B.	certainly go on be afraid
C.	I'm afraid of the dark
B.	you should be afraid of the dark
D.	what's that strange glow?
C.	that bright low light?
B.	don't be afraid of the light it's only the sunset I tell you go on being afraid of the dark
A.	should I be afraid
B.	you should be afraid there is so much threatening life

A.	what's coming out of that darkness?
B.	lung disease my friend a plague of wonderful proportions is growing in the cellars behind dark-red drapes
C.	but one doesn't talk about things like that
B.	a glorious well-trained death which manages in a tea-break to clean up the whole green-growing earth
D.	I can't help it I'm still afraid
B.	I'm telling you you should be afraid
A.	look what's that?
B.	what do you mean?
A.	can't you hear there's something moving shuffling and shambling and tramping dragging itself forward somehow
B.	of course I can hear it
A.	a great crowd tramping along what is it tramping along?
B.	it's children tramping along
C.	my god is there such a mob
D.	a hell of a life in most of them
B.	no for most of them
A.	so many of them
B.	(pointing to the screen) can't you see here they come thin hollow-eyed dumb as door posts

116

idiots with undeveloped minds
and twisted bodies
and eyes like tins of boot-polish

C.   christ what a sight

B.   look shambling dribbling limping
            what crowds of children
            bent double with hunger
            full of vomiting constipation and gut-rot
            or with ready-made education in their
              mouths

C.   they should at least have been tidied up a
              bit anyway

B.   with curvature of the spine and humped-
              backs
            tuberculosis in the spinal cord and the
              thigh-bones
            with pain in the marrow of the knee-bones
              and
            tumours growing out right and left
            what masses of children
            with full flush of scarlet-fever
            with suffocation diphtheria and measles

A.   it's horrible horrible

D.   where are they from all of them?

B.   children with chicken-pox
            children with jaundice
            children with young and happy tumours
            children with mumps and children with
              whooping-cough
            children with nervous disease and influenza
            children with dysentery and brain inflamation
            children with rickets
            children with typhus and children with plague
            children with blood-pressure and malarial
              fever
            children with cramp and st. vitus dance

	children with german measles
	children with syphilis and children black with pleurisy
	and children green and black with hunger

C.   go to hell with the children

A.   I hate your children

C.   what are they meant to be doing here?

D.   are children necessary?
for what then?
they're an inferior means of pleasure
and besides they're forbidden when they're best
and for what they're best

A.   what do we want children for?

B.   to make adults of

A.   well what do we want adults for then?

B.   don't know

A.   there you are I don't know either

D.   that's what no-one knows

C.   I won't have any part in all the children

A.   I won't have any part at all
it's a great pity for them
but more pity for us who have to stand them

D.   just think if they could die soon
immediately on the spot
just think if they all disappeared

A.   just went up in smoke

D.   if there could only be something other
                than people made of them

B.   do you mean food?

(During the 23rd speaky the screen red and the pillar
green after 'same to you' the screen dark blue and
the pillar green
The actors sit on their chairs
get up
take the chairs and go out carrying them)

TWENTY-THIRD SPEAKY

D.   well thank you very much

C.   it was really nice to meet you

B.   I think we've had a nice time together

A.   I must say it's been a long time
                since I've had such a really nice time

B.   and thanks all the rest of you

C.   thank you

D.   and thank you and you too

A.   and you too and of course all the rest of
                you

C.   good luck and good health

B.   you don't need to be afraid tonight

D.   you won't die tonight you know

A.   can't imagine your heart will break
                what would it break for?

D.	because people are suffering but after all it'll only make them better
C.	that the world is miserable what the hell do you mean by that?
A. B. C. D.	is there something wrong with something?
B.	it's only talk
A.	everything's fine and dandy
B.	and you're the tops yourself
C.	a hell of a juicy bit
D.	yes you're on the pig's back you are
A.	you're ill yourself you say
D.	you're suffering yourself you say
C.	bowed with pain?
A. B. C. D.	well we don't give a damn
B.	and besides a decent man looks after himself
A.	only weaklings need others
B.	so by-by now
C.	we'll see you around sometime
D.	enjoy yourself till then
A. B. C. D.	thanks for a nice evening
(loudspeaker)	thanks for a nice evening
A. B. C. D.	goodnight

120

(loudspeaker) goodnight

A. B. C. D.   sleep well

(loudspeaker) and the same to you.

THE END

Note for Producers:

The most important thing is to follow the rhythms of the
speakers: these rhythms and intonation patterns often take
over from lexical meaning and are a major part of the wit
in the drama. Each 'speaky' has a rhythm of its own and you
can find central shifts and changes of attitude - e.g. the
movement through admiration, the more and more angry
criticism and the surprised mollification of the poet in 18.
The lack of punctuation can make it hard to read at first,
but you can quickly find the pauses and questioning tones
(etc.) if you work with the rhythms and remember that 'O
is a creation of concepts and not of characters.' (Key-Aberg).

In the 7th 'speaky', B produces a new ticket from his
'carnet': our system is different, but I think the audience
will accept the situation without too much difficulty.

In the 14th 'speaky', the song was accompanied by a harm-
onium in the Stockholm production. In the 17th in the same
production, there was a flute accompaniment and the girl
lay more or less on top of the man.

In the 21st 'speaky', B is a sort of lonely-hearts problem-
page columnist voice.

I shall be delighted to offer help to any potential producer
if he or she writes to me c/o the Publishers.

Brian Rothwell

121

AN EMPTY ROOM

CHARACTERS

A VOICE

A

B

C

D

CHARACTERS 1 - 6

FIRST PICTURE

(An empty room)

A VOICE. An empty room.

(Darkness)

SECOND PICTURE

(One person in a room)

A VOICE. It is beneath a person's dignity to be dependent on anybody else. He should be free. He sees in loneliness the consummation of his freedom. He is happy in his freedom. (She smiles) If practical circumstances beyond his control compel him to be dependent on somebody else, he should be   for a very large sum of money. This is, namely, because he then substitutes for his lost freedom a greater economic freedom. If only he gets copious enough payment he can be as dependent as anything, and still he is going to be free.

(Darkness)

THIRD PICTURE

(Two people in a room)

HE. You smell good.

SHE. You smell so.

HE. I only have eyes for you.

SHE. Have you nothing else to offer?

HE. You're so wonderfully witty.

SHE. What's that?

HE. I love you.

SHE. What can you give me?

HE. I give you my life.

SHE. You'll get nothing for that.

HE. I don't want anything.

SHE. What else can I have?

HE. Whatever you want.

SHE. I want your heart.

HE. It's yours, it's yours. (He hands her the heart)

SHE. You don't think I can love you now, you know, you who have no heart.

HE. But darling what is it?

SHE. I can't love a heartless person.

(Darkness)

FOURTH PICTURE

(Three people in a room
A - a he
B - a she
C - another he)

126

A. Here we sit. (She sits on a wooden box with B)

C. There you sit. (Sits on a wooden box facing A and B)

B. How lovely the air is in a pine woods.

C. Cute chic. Is it yours?

A. Nice as pie. It's mine.

C. How the hell do you get hold of one of those?

A. It comes to you if you're good.

C. Is that so.

B. What's a cigarette compared to a summer day?

C. Hi, little sweetmeat.

B. How do you do.

C. Are you his chic?

B. What language!

C. He says you're his chic.

B. One doesn't own another person.

C. So you're not his chic?

B. What questions you ask.

C. Can't you try this box I'm sitting on? (To A)

A. Try the box you're sitting on?

C. Yeah.

A. Why should I?

C. I think you should try the box.

A. Do you think I should try the box?

C. Yeah.

A. Then sure. I'll try the box. (They exchange boxes)

C. Cute chic. It's mine.

A. Nice as pie. It's mine.

C. Do you know how you get hold of one of these?

A. She leaves you if you're good.

C. That's right.

B. I like the smell of men.

C. Here we sit.

A. There you sit.

(Darkness)

FIFTH PICTURE

(Four people in a room)

1. Umhm.

2. Pardon?

1. Umhm.

2. Oho, umhm.

1. Umhm.

3. Indeed

4. And how.

1. Exactly.

2. Pardon ?

1. Exactly.

2. Oho, exactly.

1. Exactly.

3. So it seems.

4. That's the truth.

3. Nail on the head.

2. Omhm yeah.

1. And that's that.

> (Pause. 4 can't say his lines because 3 has turned
> the sign around. After some prodding 3 turns the
> sign so that 4 can read his line and say it)

4. It certainly is.

3. No doubt about it.

2. The modern museum.

1. Colossal. Colossal in its truth.

2. James Baldwin.

1. Umhm.

2. Jack Kerouac.

1. Huh-uh.

2. Umhm.

3. I think it's just great.

4. No doubt about it.

1. Precisely.

2. Pardon?

1. Precisely.

2. Oho, precisely.

1. Precisely.

3. How nice it is to have a really cultural evening at home.

4. One gets so much said that one would never have got said otherwise.

   (Darkness)

SIXTH PICTURE

(Five people in a room)

1. The new man we embody is not only open and flexible and very strong, but above all fearless and perseverant.

2. He doesn't lament his fate, he doesn't shrink back under circumstances of duress: he mobilizes a large measure of self control upon confrontation with repugnant things.

3. In this manner nothing really has to be experienced as unpleasant or strange, neither catastrophic nuclear war, love troubles nor sprained ankles.

4. The new man puts his trust in renewal and is unfaithful only to faith itself.

5. Therefore it is possible for him to create an environment which prevents moral conflicts, counteracts the double standard and washes away concepts of the forbidden.

1. Greater human conflicts such as atomic wars and things, will be conceivable in principle. At the same time difficulties for the individual on a personal plane will be dispensed with, such as love troubles, antagonisms within the family and perpetual loneliness.

ALL. The constant, immense, dreaded and incurable loneliness.

2. Together we embody the new man.

3. Together we go toward the future.

4. Come, let us go.

5. After me.

1. Oh yeah, move over.

5. After me, I said.

2. After me, I said.

5. Quit pushing.

3. I'm the one who goes first.

4. That's what you think.

3. I sure do.

4. Then you think wrong.

3. You don't say.

4. I do say, because I'm going first.

1. Horse manure!

4. Horse manure?

1. Yeah, because the one who's going first is me.

4. Naw, 'cause the biggest one goes first and I'm the biggest.

3. I'm the prettiest and the prettiest one goes first.

2. I'm the tallest and the tallest is at the starting line.

5. I'm the most intelligent and intelligence goes before all else.

1. But I'm the strongest.

THE OTHERS. The hell you say.

1. But I know I am.

> (Rapidly clubs down one after the other)

> The new man I embody is not only open and flexible and very strong, but above all fearless and perseverant. I go toward the future. I go first.

> (Darkness)

SEVENTH PICTURE

(Six people in a room)

1. Oh, how wonderful is literature.

2. Man's best friend is a book.

3. There's where you find truth and goodness.

4. It's fun to read.

5. It's right to read.

6. Where do you find human love more strongly expressed than in books?

1. There's only one thing maybe.

2. There's maybe only one thing, yes.

3. Something unsound has begun creeping into literature.

4. A moral decline is beginning to spread.

5. Ish.

6. The words they use!

1. It's not the words in themselves.

2. No, it's the mentality they reveal.

3. Yes, and that threatens to infect all of literature.

4. And poison the readers who come to the books.

5. Unsuspecting, defenceless, open and full of love of the beautiful that awaits them in literature.

6. Dirty words sully the beautiful, the goal of art.

1. It's getting downright atrocious.

2. You can't open a book.

3. without smelling the awful stink

4. of a verbal and moral decline.

5. Rottenness, perversity, anarchy

6. and then these atrocious sex words.

1. It's no good.

2. It's downright atrocious.

3. It's exceedingly terrible and dreadful.

4. It's a threat against life at its very core.

5. It's goddamned awful.

1. The hell with these writing bastards.

2. These filthy minds.

3. These smut-spreaders.

4. These defilers.

5. These mud-slingers in morality's backyard.

6. These germ-spreaders of the source of life.

1. Damn.

2. Goddam.

3. Goddam to hell.

4. Goddam the sons of bitches to hell.

5. Goddam the son of a bitching bastards to hell.

6. Goddam the shitty son of a bitching bastards to hell.

ALL. Yeah, goddam the shitty son of a bitching bastards and their fucking literature to hell.

(Darkness)

EIGHTH PICTURE

(Seven people in a room.

They move in circles on the stage. Then group themselves in couples facing each other)

7. is left over, stands alone.

1. You and I.

2. You and I.

3. You and I.

4. You and I.

5. You and I.

5. You and I.

6. You and I.

7. I.

1. 2. 3. 4. 5. 6. He.

(New movements and groupings. 7 is left over again, stands alone)

1. You're nice.

2. You're fine.

3. You're nice.

4. You're fine.

5. You're nice.

6. You're fine.

7. You're so nice and fine.

1. 2. 3. 4. 5. 6. Sure.

1. You're good.

2. You always tell the truth.

3. You're good.

4. You always tell the truth.

5. You're good.

6. You always tell the truth.

7. You are good and always tell the truth.

1. 2. 3. 4. 5. 6. We are and do, yes.

(New movements and groupings. 7 is again left over and stands alone)

1. But you're a little tricky.

2. I'm not so sure of you not sure where you stand.

3. But you're a little tricky.

4. I'm not so sure of you.

5. But you're a little tricky.

6. I'm not so sure of you.

7. You're a little tricky and I'm not so sure of you.

1. 2. 3. 4. 5. 6. What's that you say, man?

7. What's that I'm saying?

1. 2. 3. 4. 5. 6. Exactly.

(New movements and groupings, now with back to one another. 7 is left over, stands alone)

1. You're stupid.

2. You're mean.

3. You stupid.

4. You're mean.

5. You're stupid.

6. You're mean.

7. You're stupid and mean.

1. 2. 3. 4. 5. 6. Now you've gone too far. You've got hell to pay for it.

(They attack him and club him down)

1. You're alive.

2. You're alive.

3. You're alive.

4. You're alive.

5. You're alive.

6. You're alive.

1. 2. 3. 4. 5. 6. He's dead. Thank god. His crime was treachery. Let's forget him.

NINTH PICTURE

(Eight people in a room)

1. My good friend.

2. My wonderfully good friend.

1. 2. Man's true nature is friendly, don't you think?

(3 comes over to 1. and 2)

1. Who do you think you are?

2. What are you coming here and making trouble for?

3. Now, now, don't try anything with me!

1. 2. Oh, so you want to fight, eh? Well, come on!

2. You don't scare me one bit!

(4 comes over to 1. 2. and 3, stands beside 3)

4. What's going on here?

3. They're giving me a rough time.

1. How can you say that?

2. What does he mean by that, anyway?

1. 2. We just wanted to shake hands with him.

3. Excuse me.

4. There. You see?

1. 2. 3. 4. Man's true nature is friendly, that's what we
think.

(5 comes over to 1. 2. 3. 4)

1. What do you want?

2. I don't know you.

3. What are you trying to muscle in for?

4. Got nothing better to do?

5. I haven't done anything, have I?

1. You never know.

2. You can tell by your looks you're a shady character.

3. Punch in the nose, that's what you're begging for.

4. I should give you a sock in the jaw, I should.

(6 comes over, stands beside 5)

1. Well, what do you want?

2. What kind of a cornball are you?

3. Shouldn't you go home and play with your mommy?

4. I don't like your looks.

1. 2. 3. 4. What if we were to give you a going over together?

(7 comes over, stands beside 5 and 6)

7. What's going on here?

1. We haven't done anything.

2. You can't accuse us of anything.

3. We just had to make with the repartee.

4. You should have seen how menacing they acted.

1. 2. 3. 4. We thought they were going to begin fighting at the drop of a hat.

7. Were you planning to attack those guys and give them a going over?

5. We just stood here.

6. They were the ones who were fighting with us.

7. There, you see?

1. O.K., don't get all het up.

2. You'd better take it easy.

3. I'd take it a little easy if I were in your shoes.

4. Just nice and quiet, you get me?

(8 comes over, stands beside 5. 6. and 7)

8. Well, well, quite a great little crowd we've got, I see, and everyone happy as a lark!

1. Well, I'll be! What a treat to see you!

2. Isn't this a pleasant surprise!

3. Old pal!

4. Welcome to our little circle.

1. You didn't think we were sore, did you?

5. Oh, you never can tell.

2. Oh, you know we didn't mean anything by that!

6. I suppose it was a kind of a mistake.

3. We were just having some fun.

7. It was kind of silly of us to imagine, anything else.

4. Now it's forgotten and turned into joy.

8. Pals, my pals.

ALL. Man's true nature is neighbourly love, that's for sure.

(Darkness)

TENTH PICTURE

(Nine people in a room.
Nine boxes with plates in falling size.
Food on the plates in the same scale)

(1 comes out. Goes along the row of boxes with the food plates on. Stops in front of the biggest portion. Sits down. Pleased and smug he begins to sharpen his silverware. 2 comes out. Goes along the row of boxes.

Stops by 1. Bends over him.

1 looks at 2. They measure each other with their eyes.
Then 1 moves a step. He now sits in front of the next
biggest portion. 3 comes out goes along the row of
boxes. Stops by 2 who is sitting at the biggest portion.
Bends over him. 2 looks at 3. They measure each
other with their eyes. 2 stands up, goes over to 1,
bends over him. 1 looks at 2. They measure each
other with their eyes. Then 1 moves a step. He now
sits at the next portion. 4 comes out. In the same
way as before, 4 forces 3, who forces away 2, who
forces away 1. The same thing is repeated when 5,
6, 7, 8 and 9 come in.

Finally 1 is sitting at the box with the smallest
portion of food and 9 at the box with the largest portion.

Then 2 looks at the food on 1's plate. He takes it.
Then 3 looks at the two portions of food on 2's box.
He takes them. Then 4 sees the three portions on 3's
box. He takes them. And so on until 9 has all the
portions)

Now dear friends let us say a prayer of thanksgiving.

. Dear Lord, in whom we trust and most sincerely
believe, We thank Three for the good he is about to
receive.

(9 begins to eat.

Darkness)

ELEVENTH PICTURE

(Ten people in a room.
They go slowly, circling around one another, observing
one another)

here! (Points at 10)

2. Yes, look!

3. How awful.

4. He's got the devil's own ears.

5. Ugly as sin, he is.

6. He's one of those who goes around eavesdropping.

7. And uses what he hears against us.

8. Dangerous, very dangerous.

9. Must be put out of the way, for our own safety's sake.

(They club him down. Then go slowly around one
another, observing one another cautiously)

2. That one I don't rely on. (Points at 9)

3. None us has such big feet.

4. First thing you know he'll begin to kick us.

5. With feet like that - one kick and it's goodbye.

6. We can't tolerate a threat like that right in our midst.

7. We're absolutely in mortal danger.

8. Not one instant will I stay here with him around.

1. He has to be liquidated.

(They club him down. Then go slowly around each
other, observing each other cautiously)

3. Watch out for that one. (Points at 8)

4. He doesn't look you in the eyes.

5. Looks dishonest, can't rely on him.

142

6. He looks to the side, that's a sign of craftiness.

7. He's working out some diabolical scheme.

1. We're not safe for one minute.

2. He has to be put out of the picture.

   (They club him down. Then walk slowly around each
   other ...)

4. Keep your eyes on that one! (Points to 7 with a red nose)

4. Ish. We don't look like that.

6. I don't trust him for a second.

1. He's so damned ugly.

2. I can't stand looking at anyone so despicable.

3. It just can't exist. No human can be that ugly.

   (They club him down. Then go slowly around
   each other ...)

5. Don't get too close to that one. (Points at 6 who is bald)

1. Under a bald head there's a sly soul.

2. It's meanness that eats away the roots of the hair.

3. He's evil itself.

4. Get him - or he'll get us any minute.

   (They club him down. Then go slowly around each
   other ...)

1. Watch out, that one's got something to hide. (Points at 5
   who is bearded)

2. People don't hide anything but wickedness and falseness.

3. Only bad men hide things.   143

3. Only bad men hide things.

4. Bad men have to go.

    (They club him down. Then walk slowly around each other ...)

2. Watch it ... a revolutionary! (Points to 4 in red hair)

3. He wants to do away with us.

1. We do away with him.

    (They club him down. Then walk slowly around each other ...)

1. That one's unnatural. (Points to 3 who is hunchbacked)

2. Then he's inhuman.

    (They club him down. Then go slowly around each other, observing each other cautiously. They stare one another in the eyes. Suddenly 1 sees that 2 has brown eyes)

1. I might have known it. Your eyes are brown. That's not my colour. You're dangerous. (Clubs him down)

    Killings a necessary evil. Now the world's a safe place for me to live.

    (Darkness)

TWELFTH PICTURE

    (An empty room)

A VOICE. An empty room.

    (Darkness)

THE END